I0080230

Digest This: Taking Ownership of Your Spiritual Journey
ISBN 978173217550-1
Copyright © 2018 by Elisia Pride

Publishing by Pride Productions

Dedication

To Isaiah and Natalie,
May you always live your truth and know
who you are in this life and the life to come.

Mommy loves you!

CONTENTS

Foreword

While reading the pages of this book, my mind was brought back to when my niece, Elisia, was a young college student. In spite of the tremendous load of classes she had signed up for, she was still searching for something greater. God had placed a deep desire and passionate yearning in her heart to strive for more of Him. She possessed this compelling determination that captivated her entire existence and would not allow her to quit until her spirit was satisfied.

My belief is that the book you are about to read was birthed out of the personal journey Elisia took to arrive at her place of spiritual maturity. God has used her to compile a beneficial resource guide for you, as you embark upon fulfilling God's desire for your life. Until you are able to "digest the meat of the Word," you will continue to fall short of God's standards for your life. As you read this awesome book, allow it to saturate your spirit man, because each chapter emphasizes necessary experiences you must encounter as you prepare for success and victory on your journey ahead.

Digest This: Taking Ownership of your Spiritual Journey is a must read for every believer. Believers must "eat the meat" of the Word in order to grow!

Today, I am proud to say that Elisia is a successful young woman, raising a family and working in the corporate world. She serves as a minister of the almighty God in the Elevation Church, in several roles. God is using her to preach and teach His engrafted Word with power and demonstration. I delight in her accomplishments and in what God is still doing in her life, and I see much more coming out of this yielded vessel. To God be the glory!

Sincerely,
Lois R. Blakes

Introduction

When my son was born, he was 9 lbs. As a newborn, his digestive system could only handle certain types of foods: breast milk and formula. And after a few months, his appetite increased to the point where he became restless, and it seemed like he was always hungry and hardly sleeping at all. Then I started adding cereal to his milk, and he became satisfied and started sleeping longer. Eventually, he started eating cereal and pureed baby food. Then he started getting teeth and was able to eat some table food. All the while, whatever was going in him was coming right out. As the food he ate had more substance, what came out of him was more potent. This was all a sign of growth and continual change. As baby Christians, we develop in much the same way. When we first accept Jesus Christ as our Savior, we can only digest simple concepts, but as we grow in the faith, we ought to be able to digest more substantial information.

"And I, brethren, could not speak unto you as unto spiritual, but as unto carnal, [even] as unto babes in Christ. I have fed you with milk, and not with meat: for hitherto ye were not able [to bear it], neither yet now are ye able. For ye are yet carnal: for whereas [there is] among you envying, and strife, and divisions, are ye not carnal, and walk as men? (1 Corinthians 3:1-3).

Too many of us are spiritually malnourished and still trying to live off of concepts that are easy to digest. Some of us don't want to grow. Some want to stay living in the familiar, living in comfort, living in our emotions, and living in a fantasy. It was never intended for Christians to just accept, receive, take in, and dwell in. We were meant to go, give, put out, and reach out. No matter where we are in life, we will always be in a season of growth and progress. If we choose to be stagnant, we will regress and risk stunting our growth.

It is easy to become a Christian, but it is not so easy to live the Christian life. Eventually, it becomes easier, but only after the concept of faith is established and embedded in our hearts. Only when the mind is transformed from using worldly methods to using Godly methods to live a kingdom life will our spiritual muscle memory be created and ingrained to the point where we don't have continual conflict between our flesh and spirit.

Philippians 2:12 says, *"Work out your own salvation with fear and trembling."* You do not lose weight because you watched someone else work out. And it is not enough to just "attend" church. Once you become a Christian and establish your personal relationship with Christ, then your growth, development, and maturity will manifest.

"For when for the time ye ought to be teachers, ye have need that one teach you again which [be] the first principles of the oracles of God; and are become such as have need of milk, and not of strong meat. For every one that useth milk [is] unskilful in the word of righteousness: for he is a babe. But strong meat belongeth to them that are of full age, [even] those who by reason of use have their senses exercised to discern both good and evil" (Hebrews 5:12-14).

We are living in a time where most people want to develop and improve themselves. We want to make our business better, develop our diet, and develop our exercise plan. We spend a considerable amount of time and energy on resources, yet we neglect the source from where we obtain those resources. Abundant living is found in consistent and constant communication with the Source of all life. Establishing, developing, and maintaining an engaging relationship with God is a catalyst to any and every area of our lives that we desire to improve. I understand why some would want to just meditate on their own thoughts because they are exhausted from having others persistently imposing their thoughts on them. I understand why people are of the mindset that there are no absolutes, and everything is relative. I can empathize with the viewpoint of a concept that is considered the absolute standard being made to fit the person instead of that concept standing alone as a guide from which to measure all other standards. People are turning inward and creating their own religion. People don't want the "religion" the church offers. It is not appealing. In this type of atmosphere, Christians who have accepted, believed, and confessed Jesus Christ not only need to know who they are, but they must also know why they believe, what they believe, and how they will live their lives according to the Bible and the personal relationship they have with God. The purpose here is not to argue or debate religion. The purpose of this book is to encourage and motivate growth and development through an intimate relationship with Christ.

My prayer is that any and every one can use this book to help develop a closer relationship with God. Too many of us still want to be spoon-fed the Word. However, when it's time to apply the Word, when the tests and trials come, we are so lethargic from just sitting and feeding, that we are not able to exercise what we have learned. This book is for those who want to intentionally and purposefully live a Christ-like lifestyle and actually take God at His Word.

Certain concepts can take a lifetime to grasp, which is why we must *"study, continually, to show thyself approved, a workman that need not be ashamed rightly dividing the word of truth" (2 Timothy 2:17).* This book is not all-inclusive, by no means, but the concepts that will be discussed in this book are concepts we will all deal with at some point in our lives. I hope the knowledge presented here can assist in equipping all of us with the tools to overcome and be victorious while we continue to work out our own salvation with fear and trembling.

CHAPTER 1
UNDER PRESSURE

When I think of life, I think of school. When I think of school, I think of its structure. Fundamentally, school normally consists of students who, for extended periods of time, are in a classroom with their instructors. In most classrooms, desks are arranged in horizontal rows facing the teacher, who is standing at his or her podium as the head of the class. The same rule applies in a music classroom. Whether there are risers for the choir or chairs for the band, everyone is facing the conductor or leader, awaiting instruction. When we leave the school setting, that same kind of structure extends into other areas of life. At work, training is normally in a classroom setting. As we attend church, the congregation sits in pews, facing the pastor, who then admonishes and instructs the members of the church. It seems that no matter where we go or what we may be experiencing, we are constantly being primed and prepped for learning.

In the school of life, however, the traditional structure of the classroom is quite different. This "life" class is not bound by a room or a specific setup. It is not filled with others who are learning the same thing at the same time, for there is only one student and one Instructor. In the case of life, this Instructor has never been taught, has never been a student, but perfectly tailors His instruction to best fit our needs. Yes, God, Who is trying to teach us every day, is our Instructor, and we are His pupils, engaged in an independent study called life.

The University of Heaven

I remember the first class I had in college that was labeled as independent study. I was expected to learn on my own and create my own tasks and goals. For this class, I was the only student, and I reported to one teacher. In this setting, where there weren't any set "rules," my only goal was to learn the subject.

Some universities defines their independent study courses as "an advanced studio course, which is not a regularly scheduled university course, but is arranged, planned, and managed by a supervising professor in conjunction with the goals that are proposed by the student, and is then approved by the professor." These universities assert that this type of course involves "more self-discipline and a greater sense of direction than do most courses." The student and the professor discuss and propose goals, topics, and projects, and an agreement is usually drafted and signed describing the course. These universities further assert that the term "independent" does not mean not "involving a teacher." *Independent* more aptly means "independent of regular class meetings," or "independent of other students." It also means students are responsible for their own work, with no one to cover for them. In other words, *I can't get by, by just showing up for class*. The final assertion of these universities, in regard to this type of study, is: "If you are self-disciplined and have a sense of your own direction and goals, then an independent study course may be a wise option. If not, think twice."

So much in life, regardless of whatever stage we are in and whatever decisions we have made to get there, means we are forever learning. There is a course that some choose to embark upon, which is an independent study. This study will assist you in every other course that you take and are currently engaged in. When you decide to enroll, the curriculum is centered on the Bible, which is the Word of God. As you study this document, your perspective changes, even though the document remains the same. You must create your goals, based on what you want to get out of the course, and have it approved by the "Professor," who is the Holy Spirit. This type of independent study must be done alone, and you must be willing to devote time to this every day. To get the most out of this course, you must consistently work toward knowing God and developing a deeper relationship with Him. Out of all the courses, this is the one that most of us desperately need, so we can get the most out of the school of life.

The goals outlined in this book are designed to examine the experiences that we all go through in life and to see how we can apply them to our particular situation. In understanding God's Word better, we understand ourselves and our situations better. I think when we realize the magnitude of God and all He encompasses, we recognize that, in order for us to know Him, we will need to invest more time, independent of church, independent of family, independent of work, and independent of all the activities that fill up our lives.

The Launching Pad

I am a busy mother with two busy children. My son, Isaiah, is an active boy who likes to rides bikes and play games, and he is heavily involved in his favorite activity: taekwondo classes. With each belt he receives in taekwondo, he has to complete a certain task. Of course, he wants to get the task right the first time he is introduced to it, but it usually doesn't work out that way. It takes practice and focus. He gets so upset when he loses or when he messes up, and this is when he's trying for the very first time. I have to constantly tell him that he should not expect perfection the first time he does something.

Like my son, when we begin to do something new or different, there is often a struggle that takes place. In the middle of the struggle, however, we must remember: **Pressure is the launching pad to our growth and development.** God uses pressure to help us change. He puts a goal in our minds, but oftentimes, we become frustrated because we are not quite there yet. It is pressure that keeps us trying, even when what's seen in our minds is not yet before us.

Our Father knows a thing or two about pressure. In the beginning of time, He commanded the light to shine out of darkness. We may not know the Bible from cover to cover, but most of us know the first few verses in Genesis: *"In the beginning God created the heavens and the earth. And the earth was without form or void; and darkness was upon the face of the deep."* Then it says, *"And God said, 'Let there be light'"(1:3).* God's command caused order to come from chaos. The darkness was content in its formless, chaotic state, but had to get uncomfortable and change so the light could come forth. Is it any different for us?

"For God, who commanded the light to shine out of darkness, hath shined in our hearts, to [give] the light of the knowledge of the glory of God in the face of Jesus Christ. But we have this treasure in earthen vessels that the Excellency of the power may be of God, and not of us" (2 Corinthians 4:6-7).

This God, who brought light to a dark situation, has also brought light into our hearts. There is a treasure on the inside of each of us. The more we know God and the glory of God in the face of Jesus Christ, God says, "Let there be light," and then we shine. This sounds great and glorious, but the truth is that God spoke a command that caused light to come from darkness. In other words, there was pressure.

Pressure Begets the Promise

Just as God applied pressure to the darkness and commanded the light to come forth, God applies pressure to us and commands His glory to come forth. In this human experience, pressure starts at birth and continues to be the precursor to all momentum, growth, progression, and increase. A mother must push to create life. The baby must push his or her way to breathe life. Our pressure has a purpose. If we don't experience pressure, we won't experience the promises that are outlined in the Word. Again, **we must endure pressure to obtain the promise.**

When I first started to feel the pressure of knowing God in a greater way, I would dream about my purpose. I would dream that I was speaking to a room full of people. This motivated me to study more and associate myself with others who knew how to study and pray. I learned all I could and spent time alone with God, reading His Word and asking Him questions. Eventually, after being established in a church, I was able to be trained in teaching God's Word. Although I have never been to seminary, my pastor (at that time) had, and He taught me (and others) what He knew.

When the time came for me to give my first sermon, I was nervous, writing everything out. Ironically, I was used to speaking in front of others, so I knew how to prepare a speech. However, the pressure came when I was asked to preach. There was so much going on in my life that I didn't have the necessary time to prepare my sermon. But I had been praying all week, and finally, after all the mental and spiritual energy I spent getting prepared, God finally spoke to me the night before I was to preach. Everything turned out fine, of course, but the lesson I learned from the pressure I felt was that God is truly in control, no matter how much effort I could give. After that, my faith grew to another level.

Pressure Cometh

Pressure comes in all forms and phases of life. We, as believers, have to be prepared to deal with it in a way that God outlines in His Word. The Holy Spirit will be there to guide us, if we choose to listen, but remember, we always have a choice. Here are some ways pressure can manifest:

Opposition: Pressure commonly comes during opposition. Before you reach your goal, there will be other areas of your life that will be opposed to this new way of living. Opposition will come as you spend more time alone while developing. There will be many distractions to deter you from reaching your goal, but when you make it through this season, your faith will increase. (See Luke 17:5.)

Doing the impossible: The more time we spend with God, the more He will reveal Himself. Then we will eventually begin to believe that *"with God, all things are possible" (Mark 10:27)*. However, when we are asked to do the impossible, we inevitably feel pressure. This type of pressure subsides when we rely on God alone; it flairs when we rely on ourselves. Therefore, each circumstance comes with a choice. God sometimes places us in these situations, so we can give up and rely totally upon Him.

Laws of the world: Pressure comes when the laws of God contradict the laws of the world. For example, there are countries in the world where worshipping God is illegal. These people have to hide their faith and worship in secret because they may suffer the consequences at the hand of the government. Ultimately, they obey the laws of God rather than man's. In America, however, we have the opposite scenario, where there are a number of things that are lawful, but they may contradict what God is calling us to do. It's like what Paul said in 1 Corinthians 6:12, *"All things are lawful for me, but all things are not expedient."* In other words, just because something is legal, does not mean we have to, or even should, do it.

Church Membership: When interacting with others, we have to know God and His thoughts about what we are doing. People have their own ideas about what they believe and will confidently express it. If we don't develop our own ideas based on the Word and our relationship with God, we can feel pressure to think a different way from Him. This can especially happen within the walls of church, if we are not careful. Many of the rules that the Church would have us pay attention to are of no concern to God. These rules, of course, are not necessarily found in the Word of God, but they are found in the regulation of church membership. Because of the rules and stipulations the Church sometimes places on others, people in the Church have perfected the role of being a good church member instead of being a follower of Christ. A member can look the part but struggle internally, all the while, the Church is busy focusing on someone's physical appearance instead of the heart. *"Man looketh on the outward appearance, but the Lord looketh on the heart" (1 Samuel 16:7).*

Take Heed

We must make an effort to remain attentive because the things that we need to focus on are falling by the wayside. Instead of focusing on money, appearance, and popularity, we should be focusing on character, integrity, and love. There are so many distractions that are in competition with the Holy Spirit, Who is trying to get us to focus on God. Oftentimes, our eyes and ears are constantly bombarded with stimuli that fills our minds with thoughts and ideas that aren't necessarily from God. We are mentally attached to our phones, making us addicted to social media, but the addiction of getting constant "likes" and "love" will only satisfy us for a moment.

We spend time on things that appear to give us what we think we need, but we often end up empty, trying to fill the void. If we are able to pass the test and get alone with God, we can begin to hear from Him about what we should be focusing on as His children. If we are able to block out the constant noise, we can learn the truth from the Holy Spirit. *"Howbeit when he, the Spirit of truth, is come, he will guide you into all truth: for he shall not speak of himself; but whatsoever he shall hear, that shall he speak: and he will shew you things to come" (John 16:13).*

Life's Pressure

Pressure brings perfection (or maturity), which, then, brings growth. Is not the reason for learning to mature and develop? Out of all the stages of our lives, it is when we are children that we endure the most pressure. Think of it: Children are constantly pressured to develop, and if they don't do so in a certain timeframe, then they are given a label, or parents begin to worry. They are pressured to talk, roll over, crawl, and walk by the time they are a certain age. Children are told to be quiet when they feel like talking or to be good when they feel like being bad. They must learn how to function in a changing body and deal with different emotions and feelings, all while listening to directions from their parents at home, the teachers at school, and the adults at church. They receive pressure from everyone around them, and this continues into adulthood.

When children become adults, there is pressure to live an adult life, to be independent and to have a job, a house, a car, and a family. The woman has been told her entire life that she will not be complete unless she has a family, so there is always pressure to be on the lookout for the man who will help her. Women feel the pressure, once they are married, to be a wife and to have children. Then, some are pressured into staying at home with the children while others are pressured to return to work.

For Growth's Sake

Because there is so much pressure that society creates, it is not surprising, as we go through life, to finally sit down with God years later and wonder *how did I get here?* The sooner we establish consistent communication with God, the sooner we will receive the resources we need to deal with the pressure of simply making decisions that are best for us, even if it's not popular or approved by others. The resources from God's Word, when we apply them, will make it easier for us to make everyday decisions. **Therefore, the more we communicate with God, the more peace we will experience.**

God's plan for us is to be refined by pressure, not to bow down under it. Pressure helps us to mature and develop and is necessary for our growth. When we feel pressure, that means there is an opportunity for growth. Regardless of our feelings, regardless of the circumstance, regardless of what we see, hear, taste, and touch, there is truth in all of this. Yes, it may be painful, lonely, and uncomfortable, but God is working in you a far more exceeding and eternal weight of glory (2 Corinthians 4:17).

Digest This

When we spend quality time with God, He begins to show us things about ourselves. Why? Because He has a purpose for everything and every situation in our lives, and pressure is sometimes how He gets things moving. His goal is to get the best out of us. However, we have to ask ourselves:

- *Am I willing to go through challenging situations in order for God to get the best out of my life?*
- *If I am unwilling, can God still get my best?*
- *If I am unwilling, will it prolong the pressure?*

By establishing a one-on-one with God the Father, the Son, and the Holy Ghost, we will be able to get the answers we look for in life, understand who we are, and discover our purpose. We will be able to know what it is that we need to do as an individual. No matter how many books we read on self-help or on getting our finances together or on overcoming emotions, nothing is going to change until we establish a relationship with our Lord and Savior, Jesus Christ. Books are a wonderful tool of motivation, but the cure to whatever ails you and has you under pressure is to acknowledge and talk with (pray to) God, Whom you cannot see.

CHAPTER 2
RAISE
THE STANDARD

Living a victorious life as a Christian requires you to live at a level that is different from the world. When we become a Christian, we are translated into a different system of operation. We are translated from a world system into a Kingdom System: *"Who hath delivered us from the power of darkness, and hath translated us into the kingdom of his dear Son" (Colossians 1:13)*. Now that we are in a Kingdom System, the standards that we had must be raised to a new standard in order to operate successfully in this world.

So many times, churches will use a worldly standard to measure success, when the world is supposed to use the Church as a standard. Consequently, church, as we see it across America, can be compared to a business. As long as the program occurs each week, the workers are in place, and the building is full, then it's considered successful. However, is it considered successful when people who have been in church for years are still wrestling with basic principles?

When you become a member of the Kingdom, the Church is more than a building. The great commission is to go, therefore, preaching and teaching to the uttermost parts of the earth (See Matthew 28:19). How are we truly going to fulfill this commission, if we are literally meeting at a building three to four times a week, looking at the same people? If you only attend a class without doing any homework, you may fail the class because you don't know the material. How can we know God by only getting in His presence while around other people once or twice a week? We've got to raise the standard. Instead of looking at the Church, let's focus inward. The Church will change as a result of each of us examining ourselves.

Foolish Things

"But God hath chosen the foolish things of the world to confound the wise; and God hath chosen the weak things of the world to confound the things which are mighty" (1 Corinthians 1:27). When I read this scripture, I think of our education system. I have learned more about life through studying the Scriptures and meditating on them than I have learned within the education system. Education

has its place, but amidst the core knowledge that is deemed necessary, there is a lot of unnecessary information. Some of it is false, and some vital information is omitted. Let's face it: many of us have learned more about history on the internet and on PBS than we have learned during our entire twelve years of secondary education. I know I can say this is true for me. My college experience was a bit more focused, but the information was still rather limited.

Learning is life-long, and if you want to benefit from a relationship with Jesus Christ, knowing how to study the Bible is necessary, though this may sound foolish to many. The Bible addresses social issues, money issues, relationships, and the history of the nature of man. It comes alive when you search the scriptures for meaning, and when you ask for wisdom from God, He reveals the mysteries to you. **You will always get a return on the investment you put into studying God's Word.**

The Cost of Separation

If you want to change the situation or circumstance you are in, it must begin with raising the standard in your heart and mouth. In this world we live in, we are faced with the enemy's attempts to come against us through media, other people, our situations and circumstances, our finances, our jobs, or our relationships. Those who are in the world are going to continue to be blinded by the god of this world until they decide to accept Jesus Christ as their personal Savior and begin a relationship with Him.

"We grope for the wall like the blind, and we grope as if [we had] no eyes: we stumble at noonday as in the night; [we are] in desolate places as dead [men]" (Isaiah 59:10). This is a picture of the average person who is stumbling through life and letting it just happen. People like this are taking in the information but not applying what they have learned. In church, we listen to the sermon, but we don't study the scriptures, so when life hits us, we are helpless. Isaiah speaks of this:

And judgment is turned away backward, and justice standeth afar off: for truth is fallen in the street, and equity cannot enter. Yea, truth faileth; and he [that] departeth from evil maketh himself a prey: and the LORD saw [it], and it displeased him that [there was] no judgment. And he saw that [there was] no man, and wondered that [there was] no intercessor: therefore his arm brought salvation unto him; and his righteousness, it sustained him. For he put on righteousness as a breastplate, and an helmet of salvation upon his head; and he put on the garments of vengeance [for] clothing, and was clad with zeal as a cloke. According to [their] deeds, accordingly he will repay, fury to his adversaries, recompene to his enemies; to the islands he will repay recompence. So shall they fear the name of the LORD from the west, and his glory from the rising of the sun. When the enemy shall come in like a flood, the Spirit of the LORD shall lift up a standard against him. And the Redeemer shall come to Zion, and unto them that turn from transgression in Jacob, saith the LORD. As for me, this [is] my covenant with them, saith the LORD; My spirit that [is] upon thee, and my words which I have put in thy mouth, shall not depart out of thy mouth, nor out of the mouth of thy seed, nor out of the mouth of thy seed's seed, saith the LORD, from henceforth and for ever (59:14-21).

This whole fifty-ninth chapter describes what it is like to be separated from God. At first, the children of Israel, God's chosen people, were following God, but gradually, they drifted away from Him. After years and generations of Israel's separation from God, the prophet Isaiah describes the nation that does not have a relationship with Him. The more they yearned for the light, the more they sank deeper into darkness. People were not looking to God for guidance, and sin had gotten the best of them. The Lord was not pleased, and He saw that there were no great men. God was stunned to find that no one was interceding, which to me, is quite interesting. Even though this chapter begins with gloom and doom, it does end on a positive note, however. God decides to intervene and save the people—not only them, but also their future generations.

Let's apply this scripture to the time we now live in. One lesson we can learn is that **when we are separated from God, we are lost, without the ability to see what we should do.** When a nation is separated from God, everyone is exposed to the threat of evil, wrongdoing, and hate. When we are separated from God, He still sees what is going on and waits to see if anyone is going to intervene. This tells me that we are living beneath our ability to affect change in the earth. Finally, it's important to note that when we are separated from God and He does intervene, He does so by raising a standard.

What Does It All Mean

Before discussing how we can raise the standard, let's first define the following words from Isaiah 59:19, including their original Hebrew meaning:

- **enemy** = tsar = adversary, trouble, distress, affliction, or foes
  standard = nüs = escape, flee, put to flight, or chase away
  Spirit = rü'-akh = the Spirit of God as an inspiring ecstatic state of prophecy; as energy of life; as imparting warlike energy and executive and administrative power; as impelling prophet to utter instruction and warning
- **flood** = nä-här' = a stream or underground streams1

Now, let's insert these definitions into the verse to reveal its true meaning:

- **"When the enemy shall come in."** It's not a matter of if, but when. The enemy can be in the form of trouble, distress, affliction, or adversaries. You can substitute any of those words in that verse, and it will become clearer.

"When the enemy comes in, like a flood." "Flood" means a stream or river that is calm, making its way. Even if there is a breach, it can still flow. The best part is that the Spirit of the Lord, or the blast of God, will lift up a standard, or chase the enemy away. This implies that God uses prophecy, spoken word, and the energy of life to chase away the enemy. We can see here how the scripture comes alive. It certainly gives us some things to think about.

In this life, there is going to be opposition. We may be trying to overcome this opposition by using our own tactics. If so, we will surely fail. We can apply the strategy of raising a standard to overcome our opposition. We are living in a time where the lines are blurred and what appears to be good has ulterior motives. To equip ourselves, there are questions we need to ask:

- How are we lifting a standard against the enemy in our lives?
- The enemy will come, but how many of us are ready to defeat him by God's standard?
- How are we to know what God is expecting of us unless we know what His Word says?
- Do we rely on what the "world" considers wise? Do we lean on our own understanding?
- Do we put our trust in what we feel is right?
- Do we depend on the preacher to study the Scriptures for us?

When you have a standard raised in your heart, then your mouth will speak.

> *"A good man out of the good treasure of his heart bringeth forth that which is good; and an evil man out of the evil treasure of his heart bringeth forth that which is evil: for of the abundance of the heart his mouth speaketh" (Luke 6:45).*

What is the standard in your heart? We are to love God with all our heart, soul, and spirit, and then love our neighbor as ourselves (Luke 10:27). How do we develop the standard in our hearts? Easy: Spend time with God and get to know Him through His Word. The more we spend time with God, the more we know Him. He will begin to reveal His love toward us and reveal things about us only He would know. When we develop love in our hearts toward God, it empowers us to know that, when the unexpected happens or when the unwanted occurs, God is there, loving us and using it all to fulfill His plan.

*****

There are three main areas of understanding that our relationship with God is built on. The higher the standard is raised in these areas, the closer and deeper our relationship with God will be. As with faith, where all you need is the size of a mustard seed, so it is with these three skills we'll explore next. Remember, you continually build off of the basic principle and raise the standard, so don't worry about trying to reach the top. It's about constant progression.

Prayer

Are you raising the standard in your prayer life? *"Confess your faults one to another, and pray one for another, that ye may be healed. The effectual fervent prayer of a righteous man availeth much" (James 5:16).*
Another way to understand this scripture is by realizing that the powerful, heat-generating prayers of an obedient, righteous person are able to get the job done.

What is the standard in prayer? *"Praying without ceasing"* (1 Thessalonians 5:17) and *"praying always with all prayer and supplication in the Spirit, and watching thereunto with all perseverance and supplication for all saints"* (Ephesians 6:18).

As you raise the standard in your prayer life, you will pray more. You won't just pray when you enter a church building. You will pray when you wake up, when you get ready for the day, when you are driving, and anytime you are conscious. **Prayer is just conversation with God**, Who is omnipresent. And the more you pray, the more you acknowledge who God is. Seeing that it is a conversation, this implies a dialogue. Prayer is not one-sided, but involves both speaking and listening. Ephesians 6:18 says we should pray with "all prayer." Therefore, let's look at the types of prayers we can pray:

- **Petition** involves asking God for something (Matthew 7:7). This is the most common type of prayer because we are always wanting or needing something. Even in our asking, the standard can be raised. At first we may ask for material things, but as our relationship with the Lord grows, we may start to ask God to change us and make us more like Him. We'll even ask for help to forgive those who have wronged us. This is raising the standard, in a prayer of petition.

- **Confession** consists of coming clean about our sins. When we first accept Jesus Christ as our Lord and Savior, we pray a prayer of confession. We admit that we are sinners and believe that Jesus died on the cross for our sins, later rising from the dead to save us from the pit of hell. However, our confession does not stop with our salvation. We continue to confess when we do things that are contrary to what God's Word says, and when we confess, God is faithful and just to forgive us (1 John 1:9).

- **Adoration** is our honor to God for Who He is (Psalm 27:1). The more we read about God, the more information we will have about Him. God is everything to many people. When Moses asked God at the burning bush, *"Who shall I say sent me,"* God said, *"I am that I am."* Colossians 1:15-17 describes Jesus as the image of the invisible God, *"And he is before all things, and by him all things consist"* (v. 17).

- **Intercession** encompasses praying for others (2 Thessalonians 3:1; Colossians 1:9; Matthew 5:44). This type of prayer is not as popular to many Christians because we are programmed to always think about ourselves. The standard is raised to a whole new level when we begin to intercede for others. It's raised even more when we can intercede for those who have not been kind to us.

- **Meditation** is silent focus on God and His Word (Psalm 1:2; 63:6; 77:12; 119:15). This is when God can speak to us using His Word. When we are away from the Bible, the Holy Spirit will bring the scriptures to our remembrance (John 14:26).

- **Thanksgiving** involves honoring God for what He has done

(Psalm 75:1; 97:12; 107:1; and 1 Thessalonians. 5:18). If some-one gives you something for a special occasion, you usually give that person a thank-you note or, at the very least, tell him or her thank you. It only makes sense to continually thank God, Who continually gives us gifts for no reason. **When we take more time to be grateful than to complain, then we have raised the standard.**

• **Consecration** encompasses committing to God and surrender-ing to His will and service (Romans 12:1). This is where we are compelled to be used by God to help others. God will show us in our prayer time what we can do to help someone who is in need. You may be praying or meditating, and God may put it on your heart to give to someone or pray for someone. This is when you help God to build the Kingdom.

• **Praying in the Spirit** involves praying in an unknown language. Because we don't always know what needs to be said, we can pray a perfect prayer with the help of the Holy Spirit. *"Likewise the Spirit also helpeth our infirmities: for we know not what we should pray for as we ought: but the Spirit itself maketh inter-cession for us with groanings which cannot be uttered" (Rom 8:26).* This type of prayer also helps us to strengthen our faith. *"Building yourselves up on your most holy faith, praying in the Holy Ghost"* (Jude 1:20). This type of prayer takes more faith because we are doing something that doesn't make sense to the average person nor to our minds. Unfortunately, there have even been people who have condemned or limited this type of prayer,

making it even harder for people to accept.
Prayer is not limited to a certain day of the week. It is not limited to your being on your knees in a room where it's quiet with no distrac-tions. Prayer can be anywhere, anytime, and in any situation.

For example, I have developed a habit of praying in the car with my children while driving them to school. We turn the radio off and often pray till we reach our first destination. When I started doing this, I always started the prayer and set the tone, but after a while, my son started praying first. He would pray for people and situations that I hadn't thought to pray about. Initially, my daughter wasn't praying aloud, but after a while, she started praying in her own heavenly language. Although we don't understand what she is praying, I assure my son that God understands all of our languages, even if we don't understand someone else's prayer. We have learned to pray regardless of the tension that we may have had before we left the house (and with two small ones, you know there can sometimes be serious tension).

We don't just pray when we feel like it; we also pray when we don't, asking God to help us through our emotions, to change the atmosphere and set our day. The benefit is that we have peace of mind. In fact, we have perfect peace when our minds are stayed on Jesus (Isaiah 26:3). I know when I have not been spending time with God in prayer/conversation. I begin to get nervous or overwhelmed, and stressed out. I start thinking that I need to handle things all by myself. It's in prayer that I can confess to the Lord my spirit of anxiety and fear, asking that He give me the strength to accomplish what I need to.

If you are not in the habit of talking to the Lord, all you need to do is start, and gradually, your prayer life will evolve, with more to talk to the Lord about day by day. The Bible says, "Be strong in the LORD and in the power of HIS might" (Ephesians 6:10). There are people in this world who are just floating through life with no one to lean on, no one to turn to—no family and no friends who truly know them. **God is waiting for you to raise the standard in your heart so He can raise the standard against the enemy.**

Study

"Study to shew thyself approved unto God, a workman that needeth not to be ashamed, rightly dividing the word of truth" (2 Timothy 2:15). We live in the age of technology, and information is literally at our fingertips. There is no excuse for being ill informed. During the Bible days, the scriptures were written on scrolls and then copied by hand. Now, a Bible can be found in almost every hotel room and on any cell phone. This is the document that we use to understand

who God is. When we get to know the Lord, we will trust Him. When we trust Him, we will trust His Word to instruct us because He is seeking out those who will raise the standard.

Think of your favorite class in school. Why was it your favorite? I would guess because you liked learning about the subject, the teacher was interesting, and you were engaged. To engage means to get involved. When you get involved in your own learning, then you will see the benefits and raise the standard in your study. Don't just stop at reading the Bible. Discover the meaning of the words in the Bible and the context of its history. Read commentary from Bible scholars using various resources. God is seeking those who are progressive, so when He does a new thing, there will be people who will go with the flow of the Holy Spirit.

Worship

When your emotions come in, let the Spirit of the Lord raise the standard instead of letting your emotions overtake you. I know what you're thinking: *That's easier said than done.* Yes, but we must let God pour out His love upon us by being in His presence. His presence comes when we praise, because He inhabits the praises of His people.

He also comes because He is seeking someone to worship Him in spirit and in truth. Worship is the most important ingredient to the Christian life. It will greatly help us to look at worship as a lifestyle, not an action. Worship is not just something we do, but it is who we are. It is a way for God to see if we are true. Worship is progressive and allows us to hear from God on a personal level. *"But the hour cometh and now is, when the true worshippers shall worship the Father in spirit and in truth; for the Father seeketh such to worship him. God is a spirit: and they that worship him must worship him in spirit and in truth" (John 4:23-24).* If God has to search for something, He intends to find it. We must raise the standard in our worship.

Step It Up

To raise the standard in our lives, we need to first ask the Lord for help. Then, we should study the Word. We need to have a solid foundation of prayer on which to build our relationship with God. **When a standard is raised, the enemy knows he can't use our emotions or circumstances to control us.** As we raise the standard when the enemy comes in, we will, then, strengthen our inner man and step into greater authority in prayer, in praise, and in worship. Remember, greater is He that's in you than he that is in the world.

Pray:

Lord, I need to raise the standard in every area of my life. First, in my relationship with You; then in my relationship with myself; next, in my relationship with my spouse; and finally, in my relationship with my children and others. I need You, Lord, to show me where I am slipping in my prayer life, my praise, and my worship. I ask that You teach me how to be better at spending more time with You in prayer. When I go to church, I desire to know how to praise and worship You with my entire being, regardless of how I feel and regardless of my circumstances. I know that when I begin to renew my inner man and be obedient, it allows You to bless me because You already know what I need.

Show me how I can advance the kingdom of God and, through prayer, destroy the works of the enemy. I declare that the Spirit of God lifts up a standard against any of my emotions that are contrary to Your Word; any of my thoughts that are contrary to Your Word; the enemy, who is trying to steal, kill, and destroy me; and any lie or curse that I have spoken or that has been spoken to or over me.

I declare that a new standard be raised in my life that will produce fruit in the areas of my relationship with You, my prayer time, my praise, and my worship. I commit today to allow You to work in me the will and the do, so I can, by Your grace, present myself a living sacrifice unto You—holy, acceptable unto You—which is my reasonable service. I will not be conformed to this world, but I will be transformed by the renewing of my mind, so I may prove the good, acceptable, and perfect will of God.
Amen

CHAPTER 3

MAKING
A DEMAND ON THE ANOINTING

As a Christian, it's not enough to just exist, doing what other people have told you to do. We are all created for a purpose, whether we call ourselves Christian or not. It is our responsibility to discover the assignment that God has intended for us.

In this chapter, I will discuss the point where every Christian should come to in his or her walk with God; it is the decision to actively pursue all that God has for you. As I said before, you will always get a return on the investment you put in, not only when studying God's Word, but also when pursuing Him for everything.

Chasing Waterfalls

Picture a waterfall where there is an unlimited supply of water being poured out. Whoever wants to receive this water can come with whatever he or she has to capture it. One person may come with a cup and drink as much as the cup can hold. Another may come with a large bucket to carry more than he or she can drink at that moment. Perhaps another person may decide to step into the waterfall and stay there with his or her mouth open. All three have access to the water and can decide how much he or she will receive. Likewise, in the Spirit, this is called making a demand on the anointing. The water is the anointing, God is the Giver, and we are the receivers. The Giver is only going to give as much as the receiver is willing to take.

To make a demand on the anointing, we need to understand a few things. According to Blue Letter Bible, the word *anointing*, in Hebrew, is mishcah (mesh-khä'), which means "a consecrated portion or ointment used to consecrate by anointing."1 To *consecrate* means to make or declare sacred; to set apart or dedicate to the service of a deity.2 The anointing sets you apart. In the Old Testament, *consecrate* is usually paired with oil, when priests commonly used it to set something or someone apart for God's use.

Anointing is also used in another context in the Old Testament. Isaiah 10:27 says, *"And it shall come to pass in that day, that his burden shall be taken away from off thy shoulder, and his yoke from off thy neck and the yoke shall be destroyed because of the anointing."* Anointing, in this context, is shemen (sheh'-men), which means fatness, olive oil, or fat of fruitful land.3 In other words, because of the fatness or fullness and overabundance of the anointing, it actually breaks the yoke that is trying to hold it. Think of trying to put handcuffs on an elephant. There's no way flimsy handcuffs can hold an elephant, because of its size. So in the Spirit, **the handcuffs of depression, anger, bitterness, or fear will be destroyed because of the enormity of the anointing.**

Declaration: I would like to take a moment to declare that you, dear reader, will come out of bondage, and its cause will be destroyed because of the anointing that is greater than the yoke. Because you are truly a Christian, a remnant—one who is the remainder, one who is remaining in the Kingdom system rather than the world's—the anointing is a part of your DNA (deoxyribonucleic acid). The anointing is in you to free you. Be free!

Our Personal Teacher

The anointing is assigned to teach you:
"But the anointing which ye have received of him abideth in you, and ye need not that any man teach you: but as the same anointing teacheth you of all things, and is truth, and is no lie, and even as it hath taught you, ye shall abide in him" (1 John 2:27).

When we understand that the anointing is within, we realize that we have a Personal Teacher who is assigned to lead and guide us. **The anointing will help us to discern the direction we should go.** When we have multiple choices before us, we can rely on the anointing rather than ourselves. The anointing will also help us to see the truth about our situation and ourselves. It reveals the strongholds that have us in bondage. Then, it seeks it out to eliminate it. This is why the anointing destroys the yoke of bondage.

Bondage is a prison, something that our minds create; the anointing destroys this prison by revealing the truth within our minds (our imagination). Our imagination is constructed from one of two systems: the kingdom system or the world system. (When I say system, I am talking about a way of thinking.) It is our Personal Teacher Who will reveal which system is truly ours.

Covered

"Behold, how good and how pleasant [it is] for brethren to dwell together in unity! [It is] like the precious ointment upon the head, that ran down upon the beard, [even] Aaron's beard: that went down to the skirts of his garments" (Psalm 133:1-2).

In biblical days, when a priest or a king was anointed, the anointing oil was poured upon him, beginning at the head and flowing down upon his beard, face, eyes, nose, mouth, and ears, covering all his senses. In hindsight, it seems like it could be a rather messy situation, but in fact, it was one of the most important acts that could be performed on a ruler.

God is giving us an image of how the anointing should be in and on us. It begins to first cover our senses and saturate us from head to toe as we are being completely covered. Why is this important for us today? It signals that our senses are important enough for the anointing to do its work there first.

As we know, our senses are the entry point for information. It is how our minds are initially exposed to the outside suggestions of the world. This is why the Word admonishes us to guard our eye gate and our ear gate so that nothing else comes in to diminish our anointing. We must continually be aware of when the enemy attempts to suggest thoughts to us that are contrary to God's Word.

The Weapons to Fight

Though we are humans, we don't fight like humans. Yes, we have weapons, but they are not ones that can be seen with the naked eye. In fact, the instruments we fight with are not of this earth, but they are powerful through God to the destruction of any mental thought contrary to His Word. These weapons, as the Word calls them, cast down our judgments and reasoning, and every barrier that lifts itself up against God's wisdom. It captivates every mental perception to submit it to the anointing.

Let's take an in-depth look at 2 Corinthians 10:3-5 to give us a clearer view on the power of our weapons in this fight:

*For though we **walk** in the flesh, we do not **war** after the **flesh**: (For the **weapons** of our **warfare** [are] not **carnal**, but **mighty** through God to the pulling down of strongholds;) Casting down **imaginations**, and every **high thing** that exalteth **itself** against the **knowledge** of God, and bringing into **captivity** every **thought** to the **obedience** of **Christ**.*

The best way to truly understand the power behind each word in these verses is to translate it from English to its original language, Greek, then back to English. Each word holds a key to unlocking the true meaning that can oftentimes be masked by the limitations of the English language.

Verse 3
walk = *peripateo* = live, conduct yourself
flesh = *sarx* = human nature, earthly nature
war = *strateuo* = to fight, active duty, a soldier

Verse 4
weapons = *haplon* = tool, instrument
warfare = *strateia* = expedition, military service campaign
carnal = *sarkikos* = animal instinct, human nature
mighty = *dynatos* = able, powerful, strong
God = *theos* = the Godhead, trinity
pulling down = *kathairesis* = destruction, demolition
strongholds = *ochyroma* = anything on which one relies; castle, fortress, fastness

Verse 5
imaginations = *logismos* = a judgement, reasoning
high thing = *hypsoma* = thing elevated, barrier, rampart
itself = *epairo* = to lift up oneself, pride
knowledge = *gnosis* = general intelligence, understanding, moral wisdom
captivity = *aichmalotizo* = capture one's mind; captivate
thought = *noema* = mental perception, evil purpose
obedience = *hypakoe* = compliance, submission
Christ = *Christos* = anointed4

Now, let's go back and read those verses again with the illumination of the original Greek meanings. We can immediately see the arsenal that God has given to us through His Word. We can also see that the war we are in is not with each other. It's not with your co-worker, your spouse, your children, your neighbor, or anyone who may have another religious or political affiliation. The war is in the spiritual places, within our minds. This is where the enemy launches his attacks. Conversely, this is where the Anointed One (Christ) and His anointing counters those attacks and wins.

Christ, Our Mind's Final Authority

Let's dive deeper into this concept of the Anointed One, Christ Jesus, and the power of His anointing within our minds. To make a demand on the anointing, the anointing must be found in you. For the anointing to be found in you, Christ must be in you and in your mind. **For Christ to reside in your mind, He must be the final authority.**

Anything that tries to enter your mind must be subject to Christ. Even though you may think it, at some point, you need to evaluate whether you are placing that thought above the knowledge of Christ and His anointing. As soon as the thought pops in your head, you have a responsibility to evaluate it and then a choice to accept it.

Ask yourself: *Is this thought from God, the devil, or myself?* If the thoughts we think are not from God, then we need to make the thoughts comply and submit to the Word of God. How do we do that? For every thought that does not line up with the Word of God, find a scripture for that thought to submit to.

Oftentimes, when a thought comes in our minds, we run with it. We begin to create and visualize a picture based on that thought. We create an entire movie that has all the parts of a story: a setting, introduction, plot, climax, and conclusion. We keep thinking and re-playing it over and over again in our heads because it captivates us, or we never questioned it when it first came into our minds.

I would often create an entire story off one look that someone gave me. Maybe I would smile at the person, and he or she did not smile back. This would set off a domino effect of thoughts and as-sumptions in my mind. I would think back to what our last interaction was and wonder if I had said or done something to offend that person. Then, I would start to be offended because I didn't think that person had any cause to be offended. The truth was that the person never saw me smile and had something else on his or her mind at the time. Ultimately, it was my insecurities that created a situation, which was not real, but was based on a thought. Sound familiar?

The Garden of Your Mind

The enemy knows how principles in the kingdom work. He's aware that **for thoughts to take root, they must first be planted in the garden of your mind.** It's God's agenda to have His Words rooted in our minds so that we can be confident in Him, making sound decisions. However, the enemy has his own agenda.

The devil has three things on his mind: stealing, killing, and destroying (John 10:10). He is always trying to plant thoughts in our heads contrary to the Word of God. He begins planting when we are young and susceptible. From there, if he has his way, he will steal, kill, and destroy each area in our lives that we have allowed him room to plant. That's why it's so important to pray for our children and to teach them the Word, which helps them combat and thwart the thoughts from the supplanter, the enemy.

The garden of your mind can be susceptible to any thought that addresses the lust of the eyes, lust of the flesh, and the pride of life (1 John 2:16). Look at your ideas about life and your opinions about who you are. You didn't just decide to think or be this way. Something was planted in your mind long ago, and it's been watered by you—by what you hear, see, and speak.

Look at a man who's angry. That's not who he is; an image was planted in his mind that showed him how and when to get angry. Someone told him, "Oh, you're just an angry little boy, aren't you?" Maybe he overheard someone talking about them, "Oh, yes he's got a lot of anger because his parents separated." Then, he begins to tell himself, *I have a lot of anger because my parents were separated. That's just who I am. I can't control it. If I could control it, I would stop being angry.*

Look at the woman who can't say no to anyone. An image was

planted in her mind that showed her how to be that way. Someone told her, "Oh, you're such a good little girl." Soon she believes she is accepted only for what she can do for someone rather than for who she is. Then she begins to tell herself, *Well, they won't accept me if I don't do what they ask. I don't want to be rejected.*

Look at the person who is always sick or who has a history of disease in the family. An image was planted in that person's mind that showed him or her how to live with sickness. The doctor tells this person, "Since you have a history of sickness in your family, you have a ninety-five percent chance of getting it, too." This person soon expects to always go to the doctor and not to live past a certain age. Then this person begins to believe, I never feel well. This may be the end. I may die like this.

Pure Imagination

A long time ago I heard a preacher named Darryl Brister say, "The mind can make a heaven out of hell or a hell out of heaven." The same goes for our imagination. Words have power, just as our imagination does. This is why the Bible wants us to cast down those imaginations that are contrary to the Word of the Lord (2 Corinthians 10:5). We must cast them down, or they will continue to play and replay in our minds. Before we know it, if we are not careful, what we have imagined to do will come to pass.

Take the story in the Bible of the Tower of Babel, in Genesis (11:1-9), for example. It describes the power of imagination. They all had one language, and they had the same idea imagined in their hearts: to build a tower all the way to the heavens. While they were building, God came down to see what they were doing. When He saw that they were unified and had one mind, He knew that nothing would be able to stop them from doing it. Genesis 11:6b, in the Amplified Bible, says, *"This is only the beginning of what they will do [in rebellion against Me], and now no evil thing they imagine they can do will be impossible for them"* (emphasis added). God knew that, because they were made in His image, their imagination had the ability to do the impossible, which gave them the ability to speak things into existence. The people were able to do what they said, but because Christ was not at the head of the plan, it was not anointed. No matter how powerful our imagination can be, whenever Christ is not the head of our plans, they will not be anointed.

Manifestation Time

God's purpose for us is to advance the kingdom, and just like a kingdom principle of sowing and reaping, the more we put in, the more we get out of it. Ultimately, He expects us to be about His business. In other words, if we concern ourselves with the things of God, God will concern Himself with us, making His anointing available in each area of our lives.

We must make a demand on God's anointing and His Word and then apply it to our lives. His Word never says, "You better worry about how these bills are going to get paid; it's all up to you." No, He says, *"But seek ye first the kingdom of God, and his righteousness; and all these things shall be added unto you" (Matthew 6:33).* Therefore, we must look at the promise, not our circumstances, no matter what our imagination tells us. It is imperative that we guard our senses and not let our imagination run away from us and become uncontrollable. I dare you to make a demand on the anointing and begin to imagine the Word of God manifesting in your life.

Examine your thinking. The only way to know if your thoughts are from God is by finding the scripture that agrees or disagrees with them. Here are common thoughts many of us have had at one time or another. View closely what the Word of God has to say about them:

I can't get anything done right unless I do it myself.
The Word: *I can do all things through Christ which strengtheneth me (Philippians 4:13).*

I think it's too late to change; the damage has been done.
The Word: *And be not conformed to this world: but be ye transformed by the renewing of your mind, that ye may prove what [is] that good, and acceptable, and perfect, will of God (Romans 12:2).*

I feel like I have lost everything.
The Word: *And I will restore to you the years that the locust hath eaten, the cankerworm, and the caterpiller, and the palmerworm, my great army which I sent among you (Joel 2:25).*

I'm not a good mother/father. I'm not a good husband/wife. I'm no good.
The Word: *I will praise thee; for I am fearfully and wonderfully made; marvelous are thy works; and that my soul knoweth right well (Psalm 139:14).*

I don't know what to do. I don't know where I'm headed.
The Word: *Trust in the Lord with all thine heart, and lean not unto thine own understanding. In all thy ways acknowledge Him and He shall direct thy paths (Proverbs 3:5).*

I'm scared of failing. I'm scared of falling.
The Word: *And I give unto them eternal life; and they shall never perish, neither shall any man pluck them out of my hand (John 10:28).*

CHAPTER 4
GRADUALLY
GROWING IN GLORY

Keeping in line with making a demand on the anointing, we need to take deliberate steps toward the release of the anointing. Just because we have something, doesn't mean we know how to use it. Let's focus on a principle that will show us how we progress toward this release.

Dichotomy: The Two Sides

Within a principle, there is always a dichotomy; two sides exists that result in either progression or regression, good or bad, growth or decline. It all depends on perception. This is what we experience in the world and how we are able to understand what we go through. We learn, at a young age, whether something is good or bad, but we also learn what benefits us and what does not. Sometimes the bad thing that happens will benefit us because we are able to define and make sense of it for ourselves, our lives, and our purpose. The principle I will focus on is subtle, but is worth emphasizing.

The Law of Gradualism

Gradual means taking place or progressing slowly by degrees. God uses the law of gradualism to build us up, to develop and fortify us. Development takes time, and the most powerful lesson the Christian can learn is how to be consistent and continual. The flip side of the law is what the enemy uses to tear us down. Gradualism, in and of itself, is not good or bad, since we can gradually progress or gradually regress.

Let's zoom out for a moment and reflect. Have you ever wondered why you are still in the same position spiritually you were in last year? Why you are still praying the same way, worshipping the same way, and witnessing the same way? Perhaps you find yourself still telling the same testimony from ten years ago on how God saved you. Maybe you are still asking God for the same thing and still hearing the same Word from God. Have you ever wondered why you are not as zealous or stirred up as you were last year, or why you are not praying as fervently, or not worshipping as much as you used to? Have you become distant to the Word, God, or the

Church? This all could be because you are not being consistent in the basic principles that initiated your love for Christ. Maybe that inconsistency is because you are operating out of emotion and feelings instead of knowledge and understanding. Maybe the law of gradualism is at work in your life—gradually regressing.

The good news is that the law works for the good as much as it does for the bad. If you find yourself going one way, you can turn things around by going in the other direction.

No Short Cuts

No person is going to hold us accountable in this individual journey. Yes, you can have prayer partners and meet at church to worship and praise the Lord in the midst of other people. However, what happens when no one is around? One-on-one time with God is where true development takes place.

"Wherefore, my beloved, as ye have always obeyed, not as in my presence only, but now much more in my absence, work out your own salvation with fear and trembling" (Philippians 2:12).

When Paul wrote to the believers in Philippi, he said that they had always obeyed in his presence, but should have been more obedient when he was absent. He went on to say that it was when no one was around that they had the opportunity to work out their own individual salvation with fear and trembling. If the only time we read the Word, worship the Lord, and pray is when we're around other people, then we are drastically slowing down our progress. The key to gradually growing and developing in our relationship with God is being consistent in the basics of prayer, worship, and study of God's Word. There are no shortcuts.

Take being physically fit, for example. If you want to get in shape and stay in shape, you will eat healthy and work out three to five times a week. You may try taking diet pills or starving yourself, or even working out for about a month. However, as soon as you stop, you will gain more weight than what you lost, thus putting you further behind in your development.

When you have a relationship with God and are growing and developing, to maximize on that development, you must be consistent—period. If you are not consistently working toward growth, you are going to indirectly work against it. As you invest your time in praying, studying God's Word, and worshipping, you will get a return of wisdom, knowledge, and understanding. As you grow in these areas, you will know the purpose God has for you.

Grow Up

God wants you to mature and be perfect, even as your Father, Who is in heaven, is perfect (Matthew 5:48). In this case, perfect does not mean entirely without any flaws, defects, or shortcomings. It does not mean accurate, exact, or correct in every detail. **Perfection has more to do with growth than with being flawless.**

> *"My brethren, count it all joy when ye fall into divers tempta-tions; Knowing [this], that the trying of your faith worketh pa-tience. But let patience have [her] perfect work, that ye may be perfect and entire, wanting nothing"* (James 1:2-4).

In this context, the word perfect, or teleios, in the Greek, means full grown and mature. You must be patient to be perfect because this perfecting process is gradual, and little by little, we grow. We must understand that there is a time and season for everything, so life will happen. However, it should not disrupt our growth and our commitment to be consistent with our relationship with God. In fact, our consistency, paired with our life experiences, will accelerate our growth.

A Time and Season for Everything

> *"To every [thing there is] a season, and a time to every purpose under the heaven: ... He hath made every [thing] beautiful in his time: also he hath set the world in their heart, so that no man can find out the work that God maketh from the beginning to the end. I know that, whatsoever God doeth, it shall be for ever: nothing can be put to it, nor any thing taken from it: and God doeth [it], that [men] should fear before him. That which hath been is now;*

and that which is to be hath already been; and God requireth that which is past" (Ecclesiastes 3:1, 11-15).

God is letting us know that there is a time for everything, and these things are going to come. The only place we can operate is in the now realm. We can think about the past and future, but we are always functioning in the present. Time can free us or bind us. If we use it wisely, we're free. If we abuse it, we're bound. How can we be free from the pressure of time? We know that whatever is coming has already come. Meaning, God requires your purpose to be fulfilled, a purpose that was decided before the foundation of the world (Ephesians 1:4). When we stop focusing on when our purpose will be fulfilled, then we become free from time.

I used to be busy. When I look back, I'm not sure how I functioned properly, with a husband, two young children, a full-time job, and church ministry that, over my lifetime, has ranged from preaching, teaching Bible study, directing choirs, rehearsing with praise teams, interceding, assisting with the treasury ministry, and assisting with the audio visual ministry. Since then, I have become wiser and have realized that, while God has given me grace to use my gifts, not all my gifts will benefit God's purpose for me. I used to push myself to get things done, even though I knew other parts of my life would suffer. I would justify it by using John 9:4, which says: "*I must work the works of him that sent me, while it is day; the night cometh, when no man can work.*" In other words, in my warped understanding of that scripture during that time, I thought to myself, *I need to work while and all I can, before I die.* It seems silly now, but how many times have we convinced ourselves (or had someone else convince us) to do something while using scripture to justify it?

Yes, there is a season for everything. I learned from wearing myself out that God, in His mercy, gave me grace to do what I did. He worked in me the will to do His will (Philippians 2:13) and gave me the wisdom, the energy, and the time to get it done. Eventually, God developed me to a point where I realized that my purpose and assignment come gradually, season by season. I don't need to know what my entire play-by-play purpose is for my life. Knowing where I should be in this season is enough. Even when I remove myself from one thing, God brings something else for me to pursue.

Slow and Steady

During that busy time in my life, I had to learn the lesson of restraint. *"All things are lawful for me, but all things are not expedient: all things are lawful for me, but all things edify not"* (1 Corinthians 10:23). Although we may have the ability to do certain things, this does not mean that God has assigned us to do those things in a particular season that we are in. Sometimes it's difficult to say no when we have the ability to do something.

Very few leaders will counsel you to slow down and take a break from ministering so you can tend to your family. Most are desperate for people to be engaged, but that engagement could backfire and lead to burn out. This is why it is important to keep consistent communication with God. He knows your limitations, and He won't put more on you than you can bear (1 Corinthians.10:13). In your communication with God, He will point out when you are putting too much on yourself. Take heed when He does. Doing more is not always better; however, **consistency breeds acceleration**. Slow and steady wins the race.

Mastering the Basics

Focus daily on perfecting the basics. You can do what God has called you to do. Don't be afraid to go to the next level of glory. God has required you to change from glory to glory to glory (2 Corinthians 3:18).

Many of us want more. We see mighty promises in the Word but sometimes have a difficult time taking the steps to get there. We won't be able to move to the next degree of worship if we haven't mastered the level that requires us to clap our hands and make a joyful noise unto the Lord. We want to move into the type of worship where we are blessing the Lord with our souls and all that's within us (Psalm 103:1), but we won't open our mouths to say *hallelujah*. Then we want to move to worship where the cloud of God's glory fills the room (Exodus 40:34), but we only worship when our favorite song is sung.

Take prayer, for example. We won't be able to move to the next degree of prayer if we haven't mastered the level that requires us to honor God, thank Him, make our requests known unto Him (Philippians 4:6), asking according to His will (1 John 5:14). We want to move into praying in our heavenly language and dispatching angels to war on our behalf (Revelation 12:7), but we spend no alone time with God in prayer. Then, we want to pray and fast according to the Word, which opens up new dimensions of prayer, hearing directly from heaven's very throne, but we neglect praying for others.

I am not writing this to discourage you. We all have to start somewhere, but the key is, we have to start. You won't be able to move to the next degree of your purpose if you haven't mastered the level of purpose that requires you to do everything to the glory of God (1 Corinthians 10:31).

We must keep progressing and gradually growing in our walk with the Lord, but it takes consistency and diligence. It is within the process that we will discover our purpose and be refreshed. Most people skip this lesson or try to use cliff notes to advance to the next level. However, in the Kingdom of God, there are no shortcuts. If we can master a daily routine of consistently speaking with God, reading His Word, and worshipping Him, we have mastered the most important level of this journey with God.

Digest This

Time for some honest reflection: Have you mastered the level you are currently in, and are you truly ready for what's next? Take a moment to evaluate what you are petitioning God for and determine if you are ready. Be really honest and forthright. (Important Tip: **Don't confuse worthiness with readiness.**)

CHAPTER 5
THE GLORY
OF PRODUCTIVITY

During my first year in college, I was so excited to be away from my parents. I was actually about an eighteen-hour drive away. I had left my hometown of Slidell, Louisiana, to attend college in Des Moines, Iowa. Looking back, now that I have children, I realize how scary it must have been for my parents to have their youngest daughter go off to a state she had never been to before, facing a different way of life in a totally different climate. However, to me, it mattered not; I was so eager to get out from under my parents' thumbs and explore who I was and who other people were.

My first year was great socially. I met so many different people, went to parties, and just had fun. However, academically, my first year was not so great. I created a major that had not quite been established at the school, which meant I needed to take more classes than the norm. (In my defense, I was assigned too many classes, but I really wasn't very focused on my schoolwork anyway.) Needless to say, I was not productive during my first semester and found myself on academic probation, in jeopardy of losing my scholarships and failing my freshman year.

When my parents found out, all I needed to hear them say was, if I didn't start being productive, I would have to come back home to live with them. What a difference a semester makes! I immediately got focused on the reason I had gone to college and ended up getting a scholarship for the most improved G.P.A. in a semester. I learned quite a few lessons from my failures and shifted my focus to a goal. In this case, the thought of living with my parents again was my motivation to get my act together. The difference between an unproductive first semester and a productive second one was my motive.

Fruitfulness

Productive is defined by *Merriam-Webster's Dictionary* as having the quality or power of producing, especially in abundance; to yield results, benefits or profits; and to be effective in bringing about.1 The Word of God has a similar take:

"And when he saw a fig tree in the way, he came to it, and found nothing thereon, but leaves only, and said until it, Let no fruit

grow on thee henceforward for ever. And presently the fig tree withered away" (Matthew 21:19).

This scripture is an example of an object that was supposed to produce, but did not, so Jesus cursed it so that it would not produce, even if it wanted to. It's obvious that the fig tree is supposed to produce figs. The verse before that says Jesus was hungry, which is the reason why He went to the tree in the first place. From afar, it appeared healthy because it had leaves on it, but as Jesus got closer, He saw that it didn't have any fruit. Mind you, this tree was growing, had leaves on it, and looked healthy, but it still didn't produce anything when Jesus needed it to. How many of us are growing, active, doing a lot of things, appearing healthy, but are not producing what others need from us when they need it most, especially Jesus?

We have to get to a point in our journey with God where we begin producing what we are made of. We are made in God's image, so we should have His same character. The only way someone can recognize if we have a relationship with God is by seeing what we produce.

Physically, our intake of food is not reflective of our activity or inactivity. So the fig tree received water and sun, just like any other tree. However, the only way Jesus could tell if it was useful was by looking at what it produced. Spiritually speaking, even though we may think we are eating the "meat" of the Word and are able to understand the deeper things of God— the mysteries and the concepts— it doesn't necessarily mean we are doing what we know to do. **We may know exactly what to do, but our doing needs to catch up with our knowledge**.

What keeps us in a state of inactivity? More importantly, why are we inactive? When we answer the WHY, we will find out the motive behind what we have been doing or not doing.

When I look at the amount of Word that has been spoken and taught in the earth, I believe that we, as Christians, should be further than we are. I'm not talking about how many church activities we are in; I'm talking about what we are producing as God's people, because we have an unlimited amount of grace.

Here are some questions we can ask ourselves:
Why am I doing what I am doing? Is it out of obligation, devotion, loyalty, duty, obedience, love, or habit?
Why am I not doing what I should be doing? Is it a lack of confidence, intimidation, insecurity, overload, over activity, busyness, or obligations?
Why am I where I am right now as an individual?
Do I have a vision of where I would like to be as an individual?
Can Jesus see the fruit of being a Christian in my life? Why or why not?

Gorging at the Table

I truly believe that we have access to too much good Word, whether in our local churches or online, for us not to be walking in total healing, prosperity, and peace. In fact, once we know the Word, we become accountable. It is like we are at this table where there is all this good food, and we are sitting there eating pasta, rice, vegetables, meat, desserts, and every variety of food. Some of us only like eating the dessert because it tastes and looks good. Some of us know we need more green vegetables, and others will just eat the pasta, rice, and mashed potatoes. Once we have the food in us, we should then have the energy to get things done. However, instead of leaving to do something else, when we are done eating, some of us sleep until the next feeding. What is the point of gorging ourselves unless we are able to burn off the calories? Back when people worked from sun up to sun down, they ate large meals, with full plans to work it off. Isn't that what food was made for, to fuel our bodies?

Why keep learning the mysteries of the Bible if we are not going to act on what we've learned? We, as God's people, have become hoarders of the Word, with very little intention to "work" it off (or apply it). Many of us are collectors of knowledge, keeping it so well hidden that we don't even remember what we have.

No Christian Points

When Jesus was out in the wilderness, people came from far and near to hear Him preach. He also baptized them. And He had a very direct response about being fruitful:

"But when he saw many Pharisees and Sadducees coming to watch him baptize, he denounced them. 'You brood of snakes!' he exclaimed. 'Who warned you to flee God's coming wrath? Prove by the way you live that you have repented of your sins and turned to God. Don't just say to each other, 'We're safe, for we are descendants of Abraham.' That means nothing, for I tell you, God can create children of Abraham from these very stones. Even now the ax of God's judgment is poised, ready to sever the roots of the trees. Yes, every tree that does not produce good fruit will be chopped down and thrown into the fire.'" (Matthew 3:7-10, NLT).

There are no shortcuts in the kingdom. Just because you show up at every revival, every worship service, and every spiritual rally does not mean you are getting any Christian points. Real change comes within the privacy of your own home, getting on your face and seeking God for yourself. Again, we have to ask ourselves, "What are we producing?"

Our prayers should be getting answered; we should be hearing a Word from God for ourselves. I would think that when we do get to church, the Word that is given to us is not shocking to us, but it is a Word that God has been whispering to us all week, and the preacher simply confirms it.

Triple A's

With all this talk of productivity, the question still remains: How do we become productive? The answer lies in the triple A's.

Acknowledge: The first step to living a productive life is to acknowledge where you are in your journey with God. You are either operating by worldly principles or godly principles. To clarify, Godly principles are principles that are in the Bible. Worldly principles are the opposite. When you begin to examine yourself, your relationships, and how you operate, you will have to get down to the root or the basis of your communication and how you function.

For example, when you've been given bad news about your health or your finances, do you become fearful or faithful? Do you deny God's power, or do you decide to believe, in spite of what you see or are being told?

Another example is your relationships, whether you are a friend, a mentor, a mentee, a partner, a spouse, or a parent. What is at the basis of your relationships? Do you put up barriers that hinder your relationships, or do you help to build and be a blessing? Are you an enemy or an ally? Are you an enabler, or do you empower others?

Oftentimes, we do things because of the examples we have been exposed to. The behavior that we have, whether it's good or bad, was modeled in front of us, so consequentially, we tend to imitate it. It is imperative that we reflect and also observe ourselves to define where we are. We must examine our everyday lives and thoughts and determine whether we are always confused or are consistent.

A lifetime achievement is accomplished one day at a time. We must be aware, on a daily basis, of what we are doing and what kingdom we are operating in at all times. *"Examine yourselves, whether ye be in the faith; prove your own selves. Know ye not your own selves, how that Jesus Christ is in you, except ye be reprobates?" (2 Corinthians 13:5).*

Ask: Once you have defined where you are or where in your life you need to operate differently, then you confess and ask God to forgive you. *"If we confess our sins, he is faithful and just to forgive us [our] sins, and to cleanse us from all unrighteousness" (1 John 1:9).* Ask God for revelation, especially if you have been deceived. Don't be overwhelmed, however. Just ask Him to reveal your purpose just for today or this week. Then ask Him to restore your joy, love, stewardship, and determination.

It's important to note that God is waiting for *you* to ask. He does not come and command you to love Him or serve Him, but He says,

"IF you love me, you will keep my commandments" (John 14:15). You have to trust God more than you trust yourself to figure it out. When you ask, you prove your trust and faith in God.

Act: The final step is to actually put your faith in action. Do something different. In your heart, you know you want and need to change. This is where you must begin—in your heart. We spend so much time making sure we act the part, but if we spend that time dealing with our hearts and making sure we don't have unforgiveness, bitterness, or resentment there, then our actions will line up with God's Word.

In the Old Testament, Samuel was a prophet who had to anoint a new king to replace King Saul. He went to the house of Jesse to anoint one of Jesse's eight sons. When Jesse brought him the first son, God told Samuel not to look at his appearance. God doesn't see people as man sees people. Man looks at the outer appearance and makes a judgement, but God looks at a man's heart (1 Samuel 16:7).

Maybe someone has made a judgement about you based on your appearance or your past, or even your current situation, but God sees your heart. It is never too late to change and do the right thing. Ask God to start with your heart and allow Him to show you how to produce out of it.

The Cycle of Production

We all have a heart, and it doesn't matter where we are in life or how much we have, we can always produce. It starts, however, with our heart, because out of the abundance of our hearts, we speak. When we speak positive (or negative) words, the atmosphere changes. When we hear ourselves speak, we change. This is the cycle of production we want to get caught up in.

As you produce, you build your faith and realize that your old way of thinking was not productive at all. It is your responsibility to produce and re-produce God in the earth. I won't assume, but I am fairly confident that most of us have experienced being hurt, whether it's in a relationship, in a family, on the job, or in the church. I personally have experienced "church hurt." Looking back, I opened myself up to being hurt when I put my confidence in man, when I expected more from people than I should have. This is how we open ourselves up to being hurt and ultimately not being productive.

As a result of being hurt, I developed an idea about church, in general, based on someone's actions. Even though I was still active in the church, instead of doing things out of love, I did some things out of obligation or competition. It took some time, a lot of prayer, and study, but eventually God changed my heart about people. I realized that **people are often unaware of what they are producing.** They don't intentionally hurt one another, but because their hearts are not right, the abundance of their hearts are being spoken out of their mouths. This is a cycle that can be broken through examination and realization.

We can't, however, rely on others to examine themselves in order to avoid being hurt. We must examine ourselves. This is how we can refrain from hurting others, even if we've been hurt ourselves.

Ask you examine yourself, ask the following questions:

• In which areas of my life have I experienced hurt?
• What is the truth about that situation? (Ask God to reveal it if you don't know.)
• When I think about this hurt, how will I choose to reflect on it?
• What have I been producing in the earth?
• In which areas of my life (relationships, goals, positions) am I not being productive?
• If I am not productive, what do I need to change?

"Being confident of this very thing, that he which hath begun a good work in you will perform [it] until the day of Jesus Christ" *(Philippians 1:6).*

CHAPTER 6
CLEAN
THE RESIDUE

There's nothing like the satisfaction of leaning back on the dining room chair after finishing a delicious, home-cooked meal. The rewards of hard work in the kitchen pay off as the tummy is now full, and the palate is pleased. At this point of delight, perhaps there's only one thought that can quickly intercept this moment: the dishes. The question at hand is do we immediately attend to our kitchen duties, or do we continue to enjoy the moment and save the dishes for the next day? Well, any of us who have ever chosen the latter knows that washing dishes that have been left out overnight is no joy, for there is a fight with day-old food at hand. However, I have a few tactics up my sleeve, especially for those stubborn casserole dishes.

Normally, I'll run some scolding hot water with dishwashing liquid into the dish. This alone won't clean it; the trick is to let it soak for some time before scrubbing. However, if I try to wash the dish right away, it might appear clean, but after running my hands across the inside, I may still find some leftover food attached. In other words, there will be some residue left behind. It will take time and focus to be sure the dish is truly clean.

As we mature spiritually in our relationship with God, we can't be satisfied with a "wash over" kind of faith. It takes time, focus, and candid examination. We need to continuously perform the deep cleaning and preventative maintenance necessary to ensure that various areas of our lives are free from the residue of our old lives—to make sure we are still in faith (2 Corinthians 13:5).

Away with Milk and Ham

As we mature in our Christian walk, there should be a point where we are no longer depending on the things of old to sustain us. We should, instead, be progressing and moving forward in the things of God. What is the point of discussing things we should have learned when we first accepted Christ as our Savior? Please, don't misunderstand; it is always important to be aware of and be firm in our foundation in Christ. However, trying to convince a mature Christian about the importance of reading the Bible, praying, and praising the Lord should not be. Those are things we should know and regularly practice by now. Why, as mature Christians in the Body of

Christ, are we still addressing (not simply reviewing) those concepts that should be easy to digest? We, my fellow believers, should be off milk by now and on to meat (Hebrews 5:12).

I'm calling all of us to step up in our everyday lives. The things that we used to let slide, we can't let slide anymore. We've reached another level, another point of no return. If we stay where we are or go back to where we were, we will not only be frustrated but also foolish. Proverbs 26:11 paints a rather graphic picture of this foolishness: "As a dog returneth to his vomit, so a fool returneth to his folly."

Purpose is key. It must be in everything we do and the reason why we do it. When we are young children, we have to be told what to do, and often without the reasons why. When we are older, however, we decide what we are going to do and when we want to do it. Therefore, if we are in a relationship with Christ, we are held accountable. When we get instructions from Him, it is up to us to follow through. Those instructions can come with a reason or not, but we can trust that when we are obedient, they will always have a purpose. The issue is when we are no longer actively listening for His instructions from season to season. We can, instead, be blindly following last season's directions, when Christ has given us new marching orders. Sometimes we can become so used to going through the motions that we don't ever think about the reason why we do things.

Perhaps you have heard the story about a woman who was showing her daughter how to cook a ham. The woman always chopped off both ends of the meat before putting it in the oven. When her daughter asked why she always did it that way, she replied, "This is the way my mother taught me to bake a ham." The daughter's grandmother soon came over to visit, so the daughter asked her why she always cut the ham on both sides before putting it in the oven. The grandmother replied, "My ham was always too big for our pan, so I chopped off both ends to make it fit." Sometimes we find ourselves doing things because we have seen others doing it, but we never think to find out why.

When we become aware of God's presence and of who we are in our relationship with Him, we are held to a higher standard, and we can't simply go through the motions anymore. When we make it a habit to think and reflect, we are, then, starting to live our best lives on purpose. This is the importance of self-examination. **When we consistently examine ourselves, we learn from our past, inspect our motives, and determine our next steps.**

A Balancing Act

Residue from the unattended areas of our lives can always bring about an imbalance, especially if those areas are not in line with God's way of management. However, there is always balance when it comes to the kingdom, and God brings it through His Word. We can use it as a guide to measure all things involving our lives.

Submission: God tells us that we should obey our spiritual leaders. Spiritual leaders will have to give an account to God for the people who follow them. *"Obey them that have the rule over you, and submit yourselves: for they watch for your souls, as they that must give account, that they may do it with joy, and not with grief: for that [is] unprofitable for you" (Hebrews 13:17).* However, there are some leaders who do not have pure motives, with the best interest of his or her followers in mind. The Word advises: *"Beloved, believe not every spirit, but try the spirits whether they are of God: because many false prophets are gone out into the world" (1 John 4:1).* The word "try" in Greek is dokimazō, which means to test, examine, prove, scrutinize, or approve. Since all leaders are not always honest or genuine, motives must be tried. There is, therefore, a balance between submitting to those who are over us and trying the spirits.

Priorities: My purpose is not to please my parents anymore; it is to honor them. My priorities are to God, then to my husband, my children, etc. I have to keep this in mind when I'm asked to do things because, even though something may be right, it may not be right for me and my family (1 Corinthians 6:12). God has purposed for us to have balance in our lives. Sure, we can have full calendars, but we need to make sure that it is full of what God has called us to do at this moment or season in our lives.

Time: This may be the most crucial area where balance is needed. Since we only have so much of it, it would behoove us to recognize the difference between the things that waste our time and the things that are beneficial. Remember, God is strategic and has divinely appointed us to fulfill a specific purpose for a specific time. He is precise and accurate, and He does not waste our time. Instead, He affirms that there is a time and purpose for everything.

From Tradition to Purpose

Concerning stewardship over the tasks and purpose God has called us to fulfill, if there are unchecked areas in our lives that we are neglecting, then we can easily become distracted with tasks of tradition. For the most part, when we are distracted, either we are not doing things we are supposed to do, or we are doing the things we are not supposed to do. Out of tradition, we can find ourselves doing things out of duty and obligation instead of love and desire to please and glorify God.

When I was a teenager, I used to be involved in church because that was what I had grown up doing. I would go to see my friends and hang out. If I learned anything, it would have been during church because I didn't study or pray on my own unless I really needed God for something. When I decided to intentionally have a relationship with Christ, the first thing God made me aware of were the areas in my life where I needed growth, which at that time, was all of them. Thankfully (and not all at once), God pointed out what I needed to do to be better. At the same time, He was also pointing me in the direction of my purpose and assignment. As each area of my life was being "cleaned," I found that my traditions started to become desires. Although I was still going to church out of obligation, I found my heart had changed. I wanted to be there. My tasks now had purpose. Realize that there is a purpose for your life, for different seasons and for specific times or places, but it requires God to show you those areas that need tending to.

Once we begin to walk in our purpose, we have to be willing for it to expand. As we broaden our definition of purpose, it may be different from where we started. In the Old Testament, Joshua's purpose changed over time. At first, he was a servant of Moses, but then he became the leader of the children of Israel and led them in conquering their enemies. (Read the books of Deuteronomy and Joshua for more details.) King David's purpose changed over time, as well. At first, David was a servant to Saul, but he later became the king and led armies into battle to conquer the enemy (1 Samuel).

No Separation

Once you find out your purpose, pursue it wholeheartedly. Stop procrastinating, and do it now. Whether you are washing food-stained dishes or folding clothes, whether you are at work, at home, or at the grocery store, in everything you do, do it all to the glory of God. Everything we do is spiritual, so there is no more separation between spiritual things and secular things. It is this truth that will help us to begin to eliminate the residue so we can be a glorious church, not having spot or wrinkle or any such thing, holy and without blemish (Ephesians 5:27). The ultimate goal is to advance the kingdom, not ourselves or our agenda. God has a plan for each of our lives every day. It is up to us to be tuned in to what He is saying.

Digest This ━━━━━━━━━━━━━━━━━━━━━━━━━━━━━━━━━

The first step in beginning to do what God has called you to do is to read the Bible with purpose. Instead of trying to read every scripture that commands you to do something, meditate on this one scripture: *"Thou shalt love the Lord thy God with all thy heart, and with all thy soul, and with all thy strength, and with all thy mind; and thy neighbour as thyself" (Luke 10:27).* If you focus on that command, the results in your life will be the benefits from it.

CHAPTER 7
DON'T RUN
FROM YOUR DEVELOPMENT

Whether we accept it or not, as soon as we say we are a Christian, people begin to take notice of our lives. It's true: **before others read the Bible, they are going to read us** (2 Corinthians 3:2). People watch what we do and who we are and then judge whether what they see aligns with what we say we do and who we say we are. This is the majority of our witness to the world; it's the way we live our lives and communicate our faith. However, when we run from the things that make us stronger, we communicate something very loud and quite clear to those watching.

If we knew what it took for God to get us to where we need to be in order to fulfill our purpose in Christ, we would not run from the circumstances, conflicts, or people whom we must sometimes face. If we knew that the job we hate was exercising our patience and teaching us skills that we can transfer to the job that we will get in the future, we would endure it a little better. If we were able to see the person we will grow into as a result of a tragedy or circumstance that will make us stronger, we would continue to have hope in the midst of the trial. Romans 8:28 couldn't be any more true: *"And we know that all things work together for good to them that love God, to them who are the called according to his purpose."*

We don't always want to believe that something bad can work out for our good, but "all things," whether they are good or bad, work as ingredients to create something good for us. This is what we need to remember as we are developing. Growth happens when there is struggle, and the struggle makes us stronger.

Hit the Gym

If you've ever gone to the gym or fitness center, you know that there is a variety of exercise equipment used to work certain parts of the body. I used to get on the treadmill and just walk, but others who were more serious about toning and strengthening certain areas of their bodies would utilize the weights. They would use them to develop certain muscles. At first, they may use a lighter weight, but as they continued to exercise certain muscles, they had to put more weight on to get the muscles stronger.

This is the principle of development. To develop means to bring out the capabilities or possibilities of or to bring to a more advanced or effective state. The muscle is inside us, but it needs to be brought out. Development happens as more weight is put on and as more repetitions are completed. When you add more weight, you develop your resistance, and when you are consistent in your repetitions, you develop endurance. So, **the result of development is an increase in your level of resistance and endurance**. What are we exercising, however, when it comes to spiritual matters?

"But the fruit of the Spirit is love, joy, peace, longsuffering, gentleness, goodness, faith, Meekness, temperance: against such there is no law" (Galatians 5:22-23).

If we want to produce fruit and be productive, we need to exercise the muscles of love, joy, peace, longsuffering, gentleness, goodness, faith, meekness, and temperance, which is self-control. The only way to exercise these spiritual muscles is by having some resistance so that, in whatever circumstance we are in, we will be consistent. Just as the weight must be heavy enough for the muscles to expand and contract, and the number of repetitions must be enough for your body to last a certain length of time under pressure, there must be weights in life that will come to test both our resistance and stamina in order to exercise our spiritual muscles.

"There hath no temptation taken you but such as is common to man: but God [is] faithful, who will not suffer you to be tempted above that ye are able; but will with the temptation also make a way to escape, that ye may be able to bear [it]" (1 Corinthians 10:13)

Love is the most important fruit to have. The Bible says that love is more important than speaking with tongues of men and angels, prophesying, or understanding all the mysteries (1 Corinthians 13:4-7). It's even more important than having the faith to move mountains. Love comes from God, and the only way we can give love is if we have love to give. We can say we love someone, **but the way to tell if the fruit of love is working in our lives is by watching our actions**. Why? Love is an action word. Sometimes it's easier to see someone else display love than it is to examine the love we display. First Corinthians, chapter 13, describes what love is:

"Love is patient and kind. Love is not jealous or boastful or proud or rude. It does not demand its own way. It is not irritable, and it keeps no record of being wronged. It does not rejoice about injustice but rejoices whenever the truth wins out. Love never gives up, never loses faith, is always hopeful, and endures through every circumstance" (1 Corinthians 13:4-7, NLT).

We can say we love someone, and someone can say he or she love us, but if the above actions are not visible in us or in someone else, then it is not love. For those of us who are being told that we are loved, but the actions of the person saying it do not line up with what he or she is saying, it's not love. That's hard to accept, but it is truth.

It's also true that we can't make someone love us. However, we can work on the way we love others. When we are in a relationship, we have entered into a spiritual gym, and most times, certain people are going to use lighter or heavier weights. Love is a full-body workout that tests both your resistance and endurance. If we are able to focus on the core muscle of love, then the other spiritual muscles will indirectly grow as a result. The main thing is that we all need to grow in the area of love, now more than ever. The world is lacking in the area of love, and if we start with ourselves, by developing and strengthening this area, then the world will be a better place.

Goes Both Ways

As Christians, there are many things we tolerate that we really should not. We've become tolerant of lying and being impatient, rude, and selfish. We've become intolerant, however, of things that make us uncomfortable or force us to be accountable. Because of our fear to face development, there are many missed opportunities, aborted purposes, avoided promises, and rejected experiences in our lives, all to make us feel better or to appease other people.

On the one hand, as mature Christians, we do have the answers and should be able to witness to others to give them the answers they need. However, we can't rest on the false sense of security that comes from our regular church attendance or even our consistent reading of the Bible, which may cause us to think we are past the need for development ourselves. This can lead us to feel as if we can diagnose everyone else's issue, while avoiding the very area God wants us to develop in.

We can go to great lengths to avoid being uncomfortable. There are very few of us who have the instinct to run into development. Some of us have moved our location so we can avoid telling someone the truth. Then, when we get to the new location, we don't want to stay because we are uncomfortable. Some believers can even begin to think that they need to change jobs because no one at their current job believes in God, and they are unable to connect with anyone. However, this may be a missed opportunity to connect with someone who is different and needs to know God. Others get divorced because of irreconcilable differences. Then there are those who stay in a marriage because they have children, two incomes, and a lifestyle they don't want to change, but they are miserable.

Development goes both ways. Sometimes we need to be still, stick it out, and learn the lesson, but sometimes we need to move forward and live the life God has called us to live. The way to know the difference is by actively being in relationship with God. At this point, no one can really give us advice on making decisions. We must make the decision for ourselves. We may make mistakes sometimes, but when we do, we can make the necessary changes and go from there. Either way, we learn and grow.

Keep the Resistance

Going back to the analogy about working out in a gym, we must understand that the key to finely developed muscles is resistance. Anytime a muscle is not being met with resistance, it can atrophy. The Google dictionary defines atrophy as to "gradually decline in effectiveness or vigor due to underuse or neglect."[1] Notice that it is the gradual decline of use (or neglect) that causes a muscle to essentially become unusable. It is the same when it comes to our spiritual muscles.

It takes work and the use of strong spiritual muscles to live our lives on purpose, and the only way to build those muscles is through resistance. If we just let life happen and allow circumstances to throw us off the path of our purpose, then we are not building our spiritual muscles. The more we resist what is seemingly going against our purpose, the stronger we become. Then, we will grow to a point where other people's opinions, life circumstances, and financial setbacks will not keep us from fulfilling our purpose or assignment in the earth. **The only person we can develop is ourselves**. We can't work out anyone else's salvation but our own. (Philippians 2:12)

If we are honest with ourselves, we wouldn't be in some of the undesirable situations we have been in if we had prohibited certain areas in our lives from atrophy. Had we kept the resistance and gotten direction from God in the first place, many of us would not have had an overwhelming feeling of being stuck. Some of us have had plans and a purpose, but because we made a choice that was not thought through, those plans were delayed. However, it's not too late. The old saying that goes "delayed but not denied" is true. If we can take what looks like a temporary setback and learn to reactivate our spiritual muscles, then we will begin to hear God's direction again to resume our journey. **Obstacles are disguised opportunities for growth**. Whether we created the obstacle or the obstacle was there as a result of life, obstacles help us to grow if we resist.

The Fruit of Relationships

Family life presents many opportunities for you to exercise your "fruit." More specifically, marriage is one of the most intimate relationships you can have with another person. Marriage requires constant use of the fruit of the Spirit. This is the one relationship where you must adjust and change in order to make it work. You can't go into a marriage thinking that the other person is going to make you happy. You must bring your own happiness ahead of time. Maybe your communication needs improvement; marriage will certainly give you an opportunity to do that. Through disagreements, you can learn how to resolve conflict in a Christ-like way without having to give your spouse a piece of your mind. In marriage, there are no secrets, and all of your flaws are visible to each other. This is a partnership in which each of you is there helping the other to grow, while at the same time, putting the other person's needs ahead of your own. Knowingly or unknowingly, each spouse will help the other develop the fruit of the Spirit. Children certainly add another dynamic to the family to help parents work-out in patience and help them develop love, self-control, and long-suffering.

For those of you who are not married and do not have children, this is why good relationships in the form of mentorship are so important. Everyone has blind spots. If you are a recluse and have given up on having close relationships with people, you will never develop. We need each other. Iron is supposed to sharpen iron. However, sometimes we try to be iron around those who are wood or plastic, just cutting them up. We need to meet our match. If iron tries to sharpen itself with wood or plastic for too long, it will become dull and lose its sharpness. Comparatively, if we have relationships with those who are not bringing anything to the table or who don't challenge us to be our best, we will gradually lose our motivation to be better. Proverbs 27:17 says it best: *"Iron sharpeneth iron; so a man sharpeneth the countenance of his friend."*

Just think of any of your circumstances or relationships that are currently uncomfortable. Which fruit are they bearing? Here's some words of wisdom: **Don't run from your development.** Before making a hasty decision to end the relationship, or change it, ask God to reveal the truth behind the circumstances.

In some cases, we may need to end a relationship because some of us are so comfortable with being the victim, or perhaps there are enablers in our lives who are stunting our growth. Maybe the enabler is you, keeping someone from developing. Whichever the case, some of our blessings are waiting to be released, but we haven't consulted with God to release the thing He needs us to let go of.

All in all, emotional wounds need to be healed. Forgiveness needs to be released. It's time to stop running from what will cause us to grow, especially if we want to see the vision of whom we can become. Let's stop masking the truth and finally face our development head on.

Take It from Joe

In the Old Testament, Joseph went through one of the most heart-wrenching family struggles to be recorded in Genesis: being the favorite child who was the object of the jealousy his brothers felt. If being ridiculed by his own father because of the dreams young Joseph was having was not enough, his own brothers decided that killing him would, indeed, still not be enough. Instead, they sold him into slavery and told his father that he had been killed by a wild animal. From there, Joseph worked in Potiphar's home and was falsely accused of rape by his master's wife. From there, he found himself locked away in prison for many years.

Although he showed kindness to the Pharaoh's butler while in prison, when the butler got out, he quickly forgot about Joseph. That alone was reason enough to forever remain in a state of disdain and bitterness, but not Joseph. As God turned his life around, Joseph found himself promoted to second in command of all of Egypt, with his brothers standing before him, begging and in great need. After everything he had faced, what were Joseph's words to them? *"But as for you, you meant evil against me; but God meant it for good..."* *(Genesis 50:20a, NKJV).* By the end of it all, Joseph embraced his brothers and fathers with open arms.

I often think of this story and wonder if I would have the courage to forgive like Joseph did—to be able to see the good in all that bad. Certainly, all of us have had bad things happen to us. Like Joseph, we, too, have to see the good in it all. People may have mistreated us, but to work out our salvation, God wants us to develop our skills of forgiveness. It's easy to run and not face it, but with God, all things are possible. *"Therefore if any man [be] in Christ, [he is] a new creature: old things are passed away; behold, all things are become new. And all things [are] of God, who hath reconciled us to himself by Jesus Christ, and hath given to us the ministry of reconciliation" (2 Corinthians 5:17-18).*

Jesus has given us this ministry of **reconciliation**, which means an exchange or an adjustment to make a difference. It is the restoration of the favor of God to sinners who repent and put their trust in the death and resurrection of Christ. Some of us have some things that need to be exchanged so that our favor can be restored. Some of our prayers are not being answered because we still have iniquity in our hearts (Psalm 66:18), or a root of bitterness has been planted in our spirits (Hebrews 12:15) Some of us are masking our pain, saying we're healed on the outside, but inside, we are barely holding it together. Let Jesus exchange that burden. Matthew 11:28-30 says, *"Come unto me, all [ye] that labour and are heavy laden, and I will give you rest. Take my yoke upon you, and learn of me; for I am meek and lowly in heart: and ye shall find rest unto your souls. For my yoke [is] easy, and my burden is light."*

People need to know that mature Christians don't always have it all together; we don't know all the answers. If we did, we wouldn't need Jesus. Jesus said that those who are whole don't need a physician; only the sick do. He also said that He didn't come to call the righteous, but sinners to repentance (Mark 2:17).

There is never a wrong time to develop because the only time we have is "now." The choices we make are shaped by what we've done in the past, but they also shape our future. Therefore, it's never too late to develop. Besides that, there isn't a finished place of development where we simply arrive, anyway.

Yes, we do, however, have milestones in life that we reach where we should be done with certain parts of development, but then we pick up a new stage as we get older and wiser. It is uncomfortable, and it can be depressing and sometimes lonely, but the return on the investment we make—intentionally working on ourselves—is worth the pain. Take it from Joseph.

John Greenleaf Whittier wrote a poem centuries ago that could not be any more relevant to our lives today. Find a place to keep this poem visible—maybe on the refrigerator, on your computer screen, or even on the mirror in your bathroom. Every time you read it, think of the areas that are calling for your development.

Don't Quit
John Greenleaf Whittier (1807-1892)

When things go wrong as they sometimes will,
When the road you're trudging seems all up hill,
When the funds are low and the debts are high
And you want to smile, but you have to sigh,
When care is pressing you down a bit,
Rest if you must, but don't you quit.
Life is strange with its twists and turns
As every one of us sometimes learns
And many a failure comes about
When he might have won had he stuck it out;
Don't give up though the pace seems slow—
You may succeed with another blow.
Success is failure turned inside out—
The silver tint of the clouds of doubt,
And you never can tell just how close you are,
It may be near when it seems so far;
So stick to the fight when you're hardest hit—
It's when things seem worst that you must not quit.

CHAPTER 8
BUILDING
A SOUND SPIRITUAL HOUSE

As we are on this journey of developing and maturing our personal relationship with God, we must make sure we have a sound spiritual house. Yes, we can compare our spiritual journey with God to that of a house. Some have taken the time to lay the foundation, build it to code, and make the house a home. Some rush through the early stages, and then when the house is built and the storms of life come, the foundation and the infrastructure are easily broken. However, if we take the time and have the dedication to build a sound house, we will not be easily shaken.

A Firm Foundation
Intentionally Laid

Our house cannot only be synonymous with a dwelling place, but it can also be an analogy for our family or our bodies. In keeping with that analogy, when we build our house, we do so by wisdom. However, we secure it through understanding.

"Through wisdom is an house builded; and by understanding it is established: And by knowledge shall the chambers be filled with all precious and pleasant riches." (Proverbs 24:3-4)

It is by knowledge that the chambers or the innermost parts shall be filled with precious and rare valuables. If we define the temple as our bodies or ourselves, then we can apply this example. On our spiritual journey of self-improvement, we need wisdom to build ourselves, and for our spiritual temples to be settled, we need understanding. Then, we fill in the innermost parts of ourselves with knowledge. This creates a stable, unshakeable person with a strong sense of who he or she is.

When we build anything, we must make sure a firm foundation is laid; otherwise, that building will crumble when too much pressure is applied. Pressure must come to test the work. We are always pressing toward the mark of the high calling, which is a result of an established, secure, stable foundation that has been carefully, thoughtfully, and intentionally laid.

Inspection Time

Ask yourself, "How firm is my foundation?" When you build the foundation of a house, there is a correct way to build it so that it stands against the elements. The house is built level so that the furniture can remain stable. The house is built with strong materials, so it can hold whatever is inside the house without anything falling through the floor.

There are four analogies to our Christian walk that we can look at as we inspect our foundation.

1. Uneven or Sloping Floors

When the floor is not level, its unnecessary parts have not been skimmed off. In our lives, this is where there are some areas that we have not dealt with, and this prevents us from having balance. We can have good qualities in our personality and intelligence, but have a horrible attitude and not get along with anyone. If we can't get along with people, then how can we lead anyone to Christ? As we build our spiritual house, we are using Christ as our model so that we replicate Him. Sometimes we have too much of ourselves in our foundation and not enough of Christ; this can cause a great imbalance. When we have a level foundation, we are levelheaded, with things in balance. Since there is no room for greed, selfishness, or pride, how do we get level? It's through God's Word. When we begin to read the Bible and apply it to our lives, it will keep us bal-

> *"All scripture [is] given by inspiration of God, and [is] profitable for doctrine, for reproof, for correction, for instruction in righteousness" (2 Timothy 3:16).*
> *"For the word of God [is] quick, and powerful, and sharper than any two-edged sword, piercing even to the dividing asunder of soul and spirit, and of the joints and marrow, and [is] a discerner of the thoughts and intents of the heart" (Hebrews 4:12).*

2. Cracks in Exterior or Interior Brick

While evaluating a house, if you see a small crack in the interior or exterior brick, this is an indication that the foundation is unstable. If there is no maintenance, the crack or cracks will start small, but over time, they will gradually get bigger. The cracks are just a reminder that we are not perfect, and we all need maintenance. Oftentimes, we go through life and ignore those little imperfections, until the character flaws grow to the point where we become unstable. I am still discovering areas in my life that I need to work on, and they are not just going to go away. Therefore, to deal with those imperfection, I need to acknowledge that they are there, and then use the Word to communicate with God about how I can improve those areas of my life. God is here for us when we are broken and bound by our inadequacies.

God loves the broken because He loves putting us back together. Our faith increases when we allow God to work on us. We sometimes think we need validation from others, but we don't have the faith to believe in God, who has validated us from the beginning. Allow God to minister to your needs first, and then He will put people in your life to assist.

> *"The LORD [is] nigh unto them that are of a broken heart; and saveth such as be of a contrite spirit" (Psalms 34:18).*
> *"For thus saith the high and lofty One that inhabiteth eternity, whose name [is] Holy; I dwell in the high and holy [place], with him also [that is] of a contrite and humble spirit, to revive the spirit of the humble, and to revive the heart of the contrite ones" (Isaiah 57:15).*
> *"The Spirit of the Lord GOD [is] upon me; because the LORD hath anointed me to preach good tidings unto the meek; he hath sent me to bind up the brokenhearted, to proclaim liberty to the captives, and the opening of the prison to [them that are] bound" (Isaiah 61:1).*

3. Displaced Moldings

When crown moldings in a house are displaced, the corners don't quite line up or come together like they are supposed to. You can see that there is a gap in the place where the end pieces should fit flushed together like puzzle pieces. Let's look at a ministry example of this.

Sometimes people in ministry are not quite gelling together. This weakens the foundation. It's like trying to cut the corners of a puzzle piece to make it fit in another spot in the puzzle. It may start out fine in the beginning, but once the puzzle is finished, every piece will not be in its proper place. This can be compared to life as well. Maybe you are in a place that really doesn't suit you. Maybe you feel out of place on your job or in your church or with the group of friends you hang around. The reason you feel this way may be because you did not take the time to know who you are. It could also be that, over time, you have changed or are just now discovering who God has called you to be. I've learned that I need to know who I am and what I can bring to the table so I know how I can contribute best. Knowing who you are is an essential part of your spiritual foundation.

"From whom the whole body fitly joined together and compacted by that which every joint supplieth, according to the effectual working in the measure of every part, maketh increase of the body unto the edifying of itself in love" (Ephesians 4:16).

"Not forsaking the assembling of ourselves together, as the manner of some [is]; but exhorting [one another]: and so much the more, as ye see the day approaching" (Hebrews 10:25).

4. Wall Rotation

This is when the foundation splits off, and the top portion turns one way, while the bottom half stays the same or turns in another direction. This happens in our own lives when we are saying one thing but doing something else. We are unstable because we are trying to accept two opposing views. We may be going through the motions at church, at work, or even at home, while our mind is not engaged. There is a saying that a company I used to work for always said, "Be here now." This is beneficial when it comes to making progress. Our minds keep us from progressing when we are thinking about the past or about things that we can't change.

"And Jesus said unto him, No man, having put his hand to the plough, and looking back, is fit for the kingdom of God" (Luke 9:62).

"For other foundation can no man lay than that is laid, which is Jesus Christ" (1 Corinthians 3:11).

"A double minded man [is] unstable in all his ways" (James 1:8).

One thing these situations all have in common is that they happen gradually, not overnight. Even though, in the natural, as pressure comes to test our foundation, it may appear to get weaker and start splitting, cracking, and moving, in the spirit, it actually makes our foundation stronger. The pressure we go through will expose and break off the weak parts, while God uses what is left to help us build and fortify so that we are ready the next time pressure comes knocking on our doors. All in all, we build faith and endurance.

"Therefore whosoever heareth these sayings of mine, and doeth them, I will liken him unto a wise man, which built his house upon a rock: And the rain descended, and the floods came, and the winds blew, and beat upon that house; and it fell not: for it was founded upon a rock. And every one that heareth these sayings of mine, and doeth them not, shall be likened unto a foolish man, which built his house upon the sand: And the rain descended, and the floods came, and the winds blew, and beat upon that house; and it fell: and great was the fall of it. And it came to pass, when Jesus had ended these sayings, the people were astonished at his doctrine" (Matthew 7:24-28).

It's inspection time. Think about your life. Can your foundation stand in the midst of trouble? Each time there was a break in the foundation, each time a crack appeared, did you allow God to repair, fill, and level you out, or did you go on with life?

Go back and review the four areas of foundational problems. What area, or areas, does God need to repair in your life? As you think about it, remember, Jesus must be our foundation. It is only through Him that we will remain strong and firm.

> *"Therefore, this is what the Sovereign LORD says: 'Look! I am placing a foundation stone in Jerusalem, a firm and tested stone. It is a precious cornerstone that is safe to build on. Whoever believes need never be shaken'" (Isaiah 28:16, NLT)*

***

A Stable Structure

We just read about the importance of a firm foundation for our lives; however, we can't stop there. **As we live and grow, our spiritual house, or structure, is being built**. Just as working out our own salvation is a continual process, the building of our spiritual structure is ongoing as well. When we accept Jesus Christ as our Savior, we lay the foundation of Christ in our lives. We receive, at that moment, everything we need in order to function successfully in the earth. As we commit ourselves daily to following Christ, we begin to build a structure that changes and grows, just as our spiritual life grows.

The Framing

In the natural, the first materials that go up after the foundation has been poured are the two-by-fours, which constitute the framing of the structure. This phase in building a house is extremely important, since all materials thereafter will be laid upon it. In the Spirit, the framing is indicative of our perception, which frames how we think, based upon our motives and intentions. The structure represents logic or an order to our way of thinking. Some of us are complex and detailed in our thinking, while others are more simplistic and general. Some of us are consistent in our thinking, while others change with every wind of doctrine (Ephesians 4:4). **Once we have established a structure, or a way of thinking, it will grow or build over time**.

Some of us don't have an issue with our foundation. We believe Jesus Christ, and we confess our sins. We make our major decisions based on the Word of God. However, we may have an issue with our spiritual structure. Some of us profess to be Christians, but don't meet the conditions of being a Christian. We play the part, but don't pray, fast, give, love, bless others, or make peace.

Digest This

Read Romans 12:9-21. Here, we see an illustration of what a Christian should look like. These deeds, which single us out as Christians, are like pillars in our spiritual house; they get fortified as we work out our own salvation with fear and trembling.

The Walls

When building a structure, there is a first phase of framing and then a second phase. In the natural, to sure up the framing of a home, load-bearing walls are added to the two-by-fours. These walls are able to withstand more pressure than the framework of the two-by-fours because the adhesive or the nails hold multiple boards of wood together. The load-bearing walls are able to bear the load of the other materials that will be placed on top of them. They are also meant for the exterior.

When we think about our spiritual house, the thoughts that make up our philosophy about life hold us up and are hard to penetrate, just like those load-bearing walls. This, of course, can be a good or bad thing. If we are thinking according to our own discretion, our structure may be sturdy and solid, but it's so solid that we won't change. It can make us blind, so to speak, to the obvious. This is how the Pharisees and Sadducees were in the Bible. Their structure was so steeped in religion and rituals that, when the Messiah, who had been prophesied about long ago, showed up, they didn't recognize Him.

We must be mindful because these walls extend well into our lives. Some of us have built our houses on the knowledge of our ancestors or on traditions. Everything we do is because we want to be pleasing to our family, or we do things out of tradition, habit, and learned behavior. Many times, we don't know why we do what we do. It's something that has been passed down from generation to generation, and we blindly continue the tradition. However, deep down we are not satisfied. Even though our actions are consistent, our heart is not connected.

Some of us have built our houses on the world's knowledge. We have to rely on books and education to teach us. This framework is forever being rebuilt because we are continually learning. Because this framework is ever changing based on new knowledge and man's discoveries, we soon find our trust shifting; this can bring about a feeling of insecurity.

When we build our structure based on our trust in someone other than God, we will always be disappointed. As we grow and go through various experiences in life, God is increasing our faith and teaching us how to put our trust in Him.

Board by Board, Piece by Piece

Anything that is valuable takes time to perfect. When we build our framework, we build it board by board, piece by piece. We don't try to finish a room with carpet, drywall, light fixtures, and baseboards until the entire framework is complete. This example reflects an issue that we can observe in a church setting.

We have people who are beginners and are just learning a concept, but before they have mastered the concept, they are given levels of responsibility that they have not yet been properly prepared to handle. How can someone pray over an offering when he or she doesn't give? How can someone lead worship when he or she doesn't praise and worship God when alone? How can someone lead others when that person doesn't have a personal relationship with Jesus Christ? These are just a few everyday occurrences in the church. We see all too often what that weight can do to someone who isn't ready to bare it. There, of course, is nothing wrong with guiding and teaching someone with these responsibilities, but it must be gradual and deliberate. Placing too much weight on a person who has yet to be *fortified* could damage not only his or her structure but also the foundation.

Fortify

The process of building the superstructure takes time. Just as the foundation must go through the testing, the structure does too. The more it is tried, the more it is refined and fortified, as each test brings another layer.

In 1 Corinthians 14, Paul talks about building ourselves up in a peculiar way. *"He that speaketh in an [unknown] tongue edifieth himself; but he that prophesieth edifieth the church." (1 Corinthians 14:4)* The word edifieth means to build a house or erect a building. **When we pray in an unknown tongue, we edify ourselves or continue to fortify our spiritual structure.**

Of course the structure does not get built in one day. Overtime, as we are consistent in our prayer, study, and speaking in an unknown tongue, we gradually build up our spiritual houses. How do we fortify, stabilize, and solidify our structure? One thing we have to remember is that we cannot do anything in our own strength or on our own. When we build our house with our hands, it is always the lowest quality. When we decide our own way, it's always the least effective way. Here are some ways to fortify our structure, accord-

Let Jesus be the Master Builder. When Jesus is the Master Builder, the structure is solid and sound. *"We heard him say, I will destroy this temple that is made with hands, and within three days I will build another made without hands" (Mark 14:58).*
Trust God's Plan. His plan for us is always going to be exceed-

ingly greater than the best plan we could ever imagine for ourselves. *"Now to Him who is able to do exceedingly abundantly above all that we ask or think, according to the power that works in us" (Ephesians 3:20).*

Use premium resources. The resources and materials that we receive from God that aid in building our spiritual house is the highest, most durable, premium quality. *"Except the LORD build the house, they labour in vain that build it: except the LORD keep the city, the watchman waketh [but] in vain" (Psalm 127:1).*

Guard your structure. We must use the tools God has given us to build our spiritual house, and the Lord will keep us. Therefore, we need to continually guard our hearts with all diligence. *"Guard your heart above all else, for it determines the course of your life" (Proverbs 4:23, NLT).*

Be Intentional

Building a solid spiritual house is a gradual process. It can be easy to fall into forgetfulness, idolatry, deception, anxiety, and doubt. However, I encourage all of us to take another look at our lives and allow God to show us the areas that we need to fortify, solidify, and secure with more prayer, fasting, and study of His word. Let's be intentional about working out our own salvation. If we have a problem with our mouth, let's study the scriptures dealing with our mouth and pray in a way that gets results. If we are being deceived, we need to ask God to open our eyes, so we can see. We need the Lord to show us who we really are and what we are really made of. We may know better, but we all need to do better, for the sake of *home.*

CHAPTER 9
PERSISTENCE

"Therefore, my beloved brethren, be ye stedfast, unmoveable, always abounding in the work of the Lord, forasmuch as ye know that your labour is not in vain in the Lord" (1 Corinthians 15:58).

Persistence is a quality that every human possess. We are innately born to be determined, and it starts at the beginning of our journey here on earth. At infancy, when a baby is unable to communicate, he or she will continue to cry until food is given or a diaper is changed. Without taking no for an answer, babies fuss until they get what they need. Some call that stubbornness; some call it hardheadedness. I call it persistence.

God has given each of us the gift to continually press onward, especially when it comes to getting His will done on the earth. He places strong desires in us that help drive us toward accomplishment. Because we are motivated with these strong desires, it is only a matter of time before we accomplish the thing we have set our minds to do.

Let's face it: if we don't have persistence in life, we will be overlooked. At the pace of this world, without persistence, people won't pay much attention to us. We live in a time where we don't have to take "no" for an answer. This is the way we get ahead on our jobs and even in our personal lives. Oftentimes, our persistence will determine whether we make the grade, get the job, or get a raise. Don't misunderstand me. I am certainly not advocating that it is because of our persistence alone that we receive these things. It is, however, a quality that gives us the edge that we need to finish strong.

P.E.R.S.S.I.S.T.T.T.

Unfortunately, too many people are not where they need to be when it comes to fulfilling their purpose in Christ. I believe it can be remedied through their desire to push, persist, pray, persevere, and endure. This must be done, even in the middle of an obstacle. I like to think of it as P.E.R.S.S.I.S.T.T.T.:

Persevere **E**ndure and **R**epeatedly **S**tay **S**teadfast **I**n **S**pite of **T**rials, **T**emptations, and **T**ribulations.

Of course, this acronym isn't spelled correctly, but it does give us an indication of the power of persistence in the middle of trials or difficulty. **Remember the previous chapter concerning growth (our development)? In order to get a fit physical body, we must exercise for more than three minutes a week. We must consistently apply resistance to our muscles to make them strong and toned.** We must jog or run past the point of simple heavy breathing; we must be persistent. It is the same with our spirit. We can't expect that attending a one-hour church service once a week is going to help us develop into mature Christians. Our walk is a daily one, throughout the day, even in the hustle and bustle of life. In order to grow, we must remain steadfast and persistent in our walk with Christ.

Persistence isn't just for our spirit, but it must be developed in our character as well. Our character tells us if we are mature or immature. We are not developing persistence to get what we want when we want it, like babies. That's what we did when we were young in the faith—crying out for God to give us our dreams, our hopes, our desires. It was more about us, which has its place. However, a true sign of maturity is persistence in doing the will of our Father—crying out for His dreams, His hope, His desires. This, in turn, leads us back to us. When the purposes of others are fulfilled, our purpose is fulfilled. Ultimately, persistence directs us to our purpose and our promise.

Faith or Fear

People can be persistent in pushing their own agendas, especially when it's not the agenda that God gave them. Some churches are guilty of this and can be persistent in getting people involved, but they don't seek guidance through prayer to know where to involve them. On an individual level, we can be persistent in justifying sin, persistent in making excuses, and persistent in coming up with reasons to do or not to do something. It all depends on what's motivating us. A lot of times, if we break down motives, we will find that we are really only motivated by one of two things: faith or fear. Let's look at the book of Nehemiah to see how this plays out.

Nehemiah, who was a cupbearer and was close to the king, heard that his homeland needed the wall around the city to be rebuilt. He prayed and received the king's blessings to rebuild it. When he went to fulfill his purpose, Nehemiah had to garnish a persistent mindset, for there were enemies who were equally persistent in trying to stop him. Even though persistence was being used on both sides of this story, it came from two totally different sources. While Nehemiah was persistent in rebuilding the wall, Tobiah and Sanballat, his enemies, were persistent in deterring him. There is a dichotomy at work here. Nehemiah was motivated by faith; Tobiah and Sanballat were motivated by fear.

Fear never comes alone; it's always accompanied by a host of sub-motives. When we are motivated by fear, we can expect intimidation, manipulation, and domination to show up. When we operate out of fear, we often try intimidating people to do things our way. It's rarely through peaceful conversations. Fear, rather, leads us to ignite negative, forceful tactics to make people do as we command. Tobiah and Sanballat did this; they laughed when Nehemiah challenged the people by informing them that they could rebuild the wall. They mocked and ridiculed the people until great sadness came over them. The two men even went as far as accusing the people of rebelling against the king (Nehemiah 2:18-19). While most of us don't openly mock and ridicule people, we will try a passive-aggressive approach in an attempt to manipulate them to comply with our demands. We offer our unsolicited opinions and suggestions that can often cause people to question and doubt themselves. Many of us will remain persistent with this tactic until people gradually cave.

As the story goes on, Tobiah and Sanballat became indignant after they heard that the people were going forward with rebuilding the wall. Their anger led them to try to manipulate the Samarian army into turning on the Jews (Nehemiah 4:1-3). After that scheme failed, Tobiah and Sanballat tried to put fear in the Jews by sending word that they would kill them (Nehemiah 4:11-12). It's uneasy to see where persistent fear can lead. It causes us to misuse our God-given purpose for our own gain. In an attempt to exert the power we feel we are entitled to—the power God gave mankind for the purpose of having dominion in the earth, not over people—we try to dominate one another. This is never God's will.

Concurrently, Nehemiah was operating out of faith, instead of fear. Yes, faith also has sub-motives, such as the mind of Christ, the strength of Christ, the power of Christ, and the love of Christ. When we are operating out of faith, our sub-motives help us fight through adversity. This is how Nehemiah operated throughout the opposition and resistance he faced from his enemies. Here are a few points we take away from Nehemiah's example:

- If we are at a point where we need direction, we begin to pray so we can get the **mind of Christ** (Nehemiah 4:1-9).

- When we are at a weak point, we call upon God so we can get the **strength of Christ** (Nehemiah 6:5-14).

- When we need to overcome the enemy, we call upon the **power of Christ** (Nehemiah 5:1-13).

- Finally, when we succeed, we remember to demonstrate the **love of Christ** (Nehemiah 4:10-23).

Who's Driving?

When we persist, whether it is out of faith or fear, we have an expected end. When we persist out of faith, it gives us the fortitude and stamina to do warfare in adversity, and we reach the victory that God promised us. We win, just as Nehemiah did. However, should we choose fear, that same persistence will lead us into defeat. Let's not let that happen. We have to push past our fear by acknowledging it. Then, we ask God to remove it so we can be motivated by faith. Remember, **persistence is the vehicle that will take us wherever we decide to go**. The question is, who's driving—faith or fear?

Some of you have questions and need answers because your patience is running out. You are on the verge of taking things in your own hands, and you've decided that you have been waiting long enough. I encourage you to be steadfast in your waiting. "How?" you ask—by praying, fasting, and studying the Word. The obstacle was created to test your motive and desires; it can also reveal where your loyalties lie.

Don't give up, though! It's time to align yourself with God and His will and be persistent. Nehemiah can teach you a lot about being persistent. Take a moment and read Nehemiah 1-6. From there, you will learn to:

- persist until you get your answer
- persist until you get the vision
- persist until the strategy comes clear and the work is complete

CHAPTER 10
FILL THE VOID
AND SEE THE VISION

When it comes to living the adult life, most of us wear multiple hats and are many things to different people. We may be a parent to a child, a director to employees, or a listening ear to a friend. Our lives are filled with various relationships, in which we are giving and receiving. Of course, if we are in the parent role, we are often giving our all for our children, and we receive their unconditional love in return. However, sometimes we give so much in a relationship only to receive nothing in return, eventually creating an inevitable void within us. As fate would have it, the person who is on the receiving end has a void that needs filling just as much as the giver does.

One thing I have learned about myself is that only God can fill the empty places in my life. **The void we desire other people to fill in us won't ever be filled**. The efforts of others will never satisfy. Just as a gas tank must be filled with gasoline in order to fuel a vehicle, we must be filled with God, so our spiritual tank can be full. This is contingent on developing a relationship with God.

Prior to having a relationship with Christ, we continually attempt to fill our own voids. If we don't receive enough love, attention, or direction from those we expect to love us the most, then we begin to search for something that will fill that void. Our desire is to be whole, and once we discover Jesus, we gradually discover that He is everything that we need.

The Origin Story

The places where we feel most empty can be traced back to the origins of our childhood. I observe my children's personalities often, and they are like night and day. My son thinks he's always being cheated, feeling like his younger sister has more than he does. He's always comparing himself to her. I often remind him that he had us all to himself for three years and didn't have to compete for our attention like his sister does. I tell him that she may have more of *this*, but he has other things that she doesn't because she's too young. I explain that he is older and needs to set a good example for her. Until my son develops a relationship with God and discovers who he is in Christ, he will continue to compare himself to his sister, believing that he needs to have more than she has.

My son wasn't the only one in the family who needed a *filling* from the Lord. I had my own personal challenges that I had to work through. My tendency to depend on others to fill what only God could was in need of attention. I used to give to get something in return, only to find that when I didn't receive it, I would feel hurt. The giving was not the problem; it was the motive and need behind the giving that was the issue. You see, I placed the responsibility on others to meet a deep need in my soul; however, it is not the job of others to give what only God can. He had to heal the fracture in my soul that had been created by those empty places within. The parts I thought my parents were supposed to fill, that having children should fill, and the parts I thought money would fill, all ended up failing to fill those empty areas that only God could touch. My demands on my parents, children, and money were too great for them to bear. Only God has the strength to bear such a weight.

So how do we move toward filling the voids that are in our lives so we can be, as James 1:4 says, "complete and entire, wanting nothing"? First, we need to acknowledge that there is a void, and that what (or whom, in some cases) we are trying to fill it with will not suffice.

Lose to Gain

Self-evaluation is key if we want to locate the voids in our lives. In other words, we need to identify, take inventory, and evaluate what we know about ourselves. Of course, it's better to do such an assessment when life is quiet and all is well; however, quiet is not always what life gives us. Many times, we are able to identify a void when loss occurs—loss of material possessions, of a loved one, or even of a relationship. Unfortunately, sometimes it takes going through a traumatic experience to realize that there is something in us that is empty, especially if that something has been occupying a deep personal space within us. It's harder to identify these voids when we believe they are being filled. One way to identify such an area is by asking ourselves what is the one thing or person that, if taken away, would create such a devastating loss that we wouldn't be able to function.

In Matthew, chapter 19, a rich, young ruler asked Jesus what he needed to do to have eternal life. Jesus answered saying that he needed to keep the commandments. The man asked which ones. Jesus then told him that he must not murder, commit adultery, steal, or lie, and to honor his father and mother, loving his neighbor as he loves himself. The man said that he had been obeying these commandments since he was a child. The young ruler could have stopped there and thanked Jesus, thinking all is well with him. But he probed further and asked Jesus the most important question: *"What else must I do?" (Matthew 19:20, NLT)*. Jesus lovingly answered the young man with something the young man did not want to hear. *"If you want to be perfect, go and sell all your possessions and give the money to the poor, and you will have treasure in heaven. Then come, follow me" (Matthew 19:21, NLT)*. When the man heard this, he walked away sad, because he had many possessions. More importantly, many possessions had him.

One of the lessons of maturity is to be ready to lose in order to gain. We can learn from this example how we should approach identifying our void. We can ask God what else we can do. When we have taken the time to pray, study, and spend time with Him, and we feel we are in a good place in our spirituality, we can ask, what else, God? We should be prepared for an answer. God's response will certainly help us to grow to the point where we are perfect and entire, wanting nothing.

Ask, Seek, Find

God is the source, and everything else is a resource. Everything that we need will come from Him. We spend too much time trying to figure out how to fill our own voids instead of consulting with the Source—God.

> *Ask, and it shall be given you; seek, and ye shall find; knock, and it shall be opened unto you: For every one that asketh receiveth; and he that seeketh findeth; and to him that knocketh it shall be opened. Or what man is there of you, whom if his son ask bread, will he give him a stone? Or if he ask a fish, will he give him a ser-pent? If ye then, being evil, know how to give good gifts unto your*

children, how much more shall your Father which is in heaven give good things to them that ask him? (Matthew 7:7-11).

When we are trying to figure something out, these verses in Matthew tell us what to do to solve our problem. First, we ask, expecting for it to be given. Of course, God is not a genie in a bottle. We have to ask according to His Word, with pure motives and intentions. The implication here is that we receive what is being given when we ask. The assumption is that we are in need of something. *"Ye ask, and receive not, because ye ask amiss, that ye may consume [it] upon your lusts" (James 4:3).*

From time to time, we ask for things that we don't need, sometimes for the wrong reasons. Thankfully, God is not looking at our minds and what we think we want, but He is seeing our heart and determining what we need. (To be honest, I'm glad that some of my prayers weren't answered.) When we are examining ourselves, we ask questions that cause us to grow closer to God. Then He will give us the answer. When He gives us the answer, however, we must decide whether we want to receive it or walk away.

The next part of this scripture says to seek, and you will find it. The assumption is that we have lost something. God knew and created us before we were in our mother's womb (Jeremiah 1:5). He placed everything in us that we need to function and to be successful in the earth. When we are born, we forget, but when we decide to accept Jesus as our personal Savior, then He begins to show us who we are in Him. **As we seek God, we find ourselves**.

The third part says to knock, and it will be opened. Here, a door is being implied. We can knock so hard that the door opens, but until we actually walk through, we will stay where we are. I think the door represents the new. Whether it's a new chapter in our lives, a new perspective, or a new revelation, once we walk through the door, we don't go back. Then, there are more doors to be opened so that we can keep choosing to walk though those doors and continue moving forward.

The Full Vision

Once we identify the void, then it needs to be filled. Habakkuk 2:1-4 says:

I will stand upon my watch, and set me upon the tower, and will watch to see what he will say unto me, and what I shall answer when I am reproved. And the LORD answered me, and said, Write the vision, and make [it] plain upon tables, that he may run that readeth it. For the vision [is] yet for an appointed time, but at the end it shall speak, and not lie: though it tarry, wait for it; because it will surely come, it will not tarry. Behold, his soul [which] is lifted up is not upright in him: but the just shall live by his faith.

Vision is something we will have as a result of spending time with God. As we spend time with Him, we are gradually recognizing various voids in our lives, while God gradually fills them. He does this by giving us a vision of our future.

There are lots of things in our lives that we want to achieve but have yet to do so. We may want to be debt free and have a healthy life, with healthy relationships. This won't just happen. We have to envision our fullness.

A lot of people work hard to have fullness in their lives. If you have been working all of your life and still are not producing the fruit that you desire, then look closely at the scripture above. The first thing the prophet did was seek the Lord and wait to hear a word from Him. Then, the Lord answered and directed him to write the vision. The Lord went on to advise that the vision is for an appointed time. Even though it takes time, we must wait for it because, at the right moment, it will happen. However, God gives us a key: the just must live by faith. If we don't live by faith, like we already know it will be done, then we will live anxiously or fretfully in the unknown.

Others

God is a void-filler. Having a relationship with Jesus Christ automatically fills the void in our lives. As we wait to hear from the

Lord in prayer, we develop Christ-like attributes that bring us closer to fulfilling our purpose in Him. Instead of looking at what we want to fill the void, we should be courageous enough to look for the attributes that we are missing so that we can produce these things in our lives. We develop stewardship to manage our money and our time properly. We attain wisdom to be able to make good decisions in life. We develop consistency so we can be a trusted witness to others in the earth.

God wants to restore us so we can restore others. If we are all walking around with pockets of emptiness, then how will we be able to help others? Some of us have deep voids that need a deep filling, so let's begin the healing process. After we've identified our void, let's stop replacing those empty places with people or things and ask God to fill our hearts and minds so we can live in a place of fullness, wholeness, and completeness.

Let's start today by asking God to fill those empty places and to reveal the vision He has for our lives. Don't know where to begin? Start here:

Prayer
Lord, fill the empty places in my past. Restore the void that past relationships have caused. Help me to stop replacing the empty places with people or things. I need You, Lord, to fill up my empty places. Fill the bank of my heart, mind, future, and destiny. Help me to envision my fullness, beginning with envisioning who You are. Help me to continually identify the empty places. I seek guidance from You, Lord, and receive love from You so I can begin to heal from those places that have been empty for so long. Show me the void that is in my life, and show me what else I must do. I seek and thirst after Your Word. I declare that You are bringing me to a place of fullness, wholeness, and completeness. I am expecting You to fill me to overflow and to make me complete and whole again.

In Jesus' name I pray,

Amen

CHAPTER 11
UNFILTERED
WORSHIP

John 4:24 says, *"God is a Spirit: and they that worship him must worship him in spirit and in truth."* Worship is the most important ingredient in the Christian life. We know that, when we first become a Christian, it is because we accept Jesus as our Savior, admitting that we have sinned and that Jesus died for our sins (Romans 10:9). We know Philippians 2:12 says, *"Wherefore, my beloved, as ye have always obeyed, not as in my presence only, but now much more in my absence, work out your own salvation with fear and trembling."* However, we don't simply stop at accepting and believing; there is action that must follow. Every time we choose to obey God, it's a form of worship. Yet, it does not stop with obedience alone. Worship is who we are, not just merely the actions we take here and there. **Worship is a lifestyle that we live every day**.

Try Worship

When we worship, it shows God that we are true and in the Spirit. To demystify what *true worship in the Spirit* means, think of it as a personal expression from an authentic place within our spirits. Essentially, we have to forget about what everyone else is doing, because worship is personal. It is a sacrifice that takes our whole being. Worship is progressive and allows us to hear from God on an individual level. Often, in our alone time with God, we spend so much of it trying to figure out our own problems and trying to solve other people's issues, but God wants and is seeking people who will come and worship Him.

Let's go to the Word and look at John, chapter 4. Specifically, let's look at verses 23 and 24:

"But the hour cometh, and now is, when the true worshippers shall worship the Father in spirit and in truth; for the Father seeketh such to worship him. God is a spirit: and they that worship him must worship him in spirit and in truth. "

What does this mean? Worship is a vehicle through which we access God. When nothing else has worked, Jesus admonishes us, with His own words, to try worship. Oftentimes, life comes at us strongly, so we must be equipped for it.

- When the doctor does not give you a good report, try worship.
- When something or someone has made you angry, try worship.
- When you feel like you can't handle life and are overwhelmed, try worship.

Worship must be a priority in the Christian life, especially if God the Father is seeking true worshippers. If God has to seek or search, the implication is that He hasn't found it. It also implies that what some of us think is worship may not be. If the scripture says that true worshippers shall worship the Father in Spirit and in truth, then there must be a disheartening reality—false worshippers are among us.

Well, Well, Well

Everyone has an individual walk, with individual perspectives. When external information comes in, we filter it based on our perception. Take a camera lens that can be used to take photos. The look of the picture will change based on the filter that is applied to it. As the filter changes, the picture changes. So it is with us. We have filters such as our past, our logic, our prejudices, and our judgments that we apply to situations throughout our lives. We hear the Word, but the filter we have placed on it will determine our perspective regarding it. We worship, but our filter will alter it. The only filter we need on our worship and the Word is that of Spirit and truth.

Going back to the passage in John 4, let's look at the filters that were holding this Samaritan woman back from true worship in the Spirit and see how we can apply it to our lives. In the first few verses of chapter 4, Jesus has left Judaea to go to Galilee, but He first has to go through Samaria. The Bible says, *"And he must needs go through Samaria" (John 4:4).* It must have been a very important assignment for Him to go through Samaria. This was not a place where most Jews wanted to go, due to the cultural and social differences between Jews and Samaritans. There was a well on the land that had previously been owned by Jacob's lineage. Essentially, there was a history of covenant and promises associated with this land. When Jesus stops to rest, a Samaritan woman comes to draw water from the well.

"Jesus saith unto her, Give me to drink. (For his disciples were gone away unto the city to buy meat)" (vv. 7b-8).

It is important to note that this was a highly unlikely interaction between a rabbi and a woman with a salacious past. However, Jesus was not a typical rabbi. He made sure their conversation would not be overheard by other people who may have judged, condemned, or criticized her situation. Jesus didn't filter this circumstance with judgment; He filtered it with compassion. **God desires to get us alone so that we don't feel the pressure or judgment from others**, which can sometimes take place in our own minds.

"Then saith the woman of Samaria unto him, How is it that thou, being a Jew, askest drink of me, which am a woman of Samaria? for the Jews have no dealings with the Samaritans" (v. 9).

We now see her filter of prejudice showing up. Yes, it was widely known that the Jews had no dealings with the Samaritans. Jesus, nonetheless, tries to have a private conversation with her and asks her to do something for Him. In effect, Jesus tries to engage her in a personal and private worship experience. However, the Samaritan woman is focused on the social rules of the day, which penetrate her mindset in the form of prejudice. Does this sound familiar?

We all have prejudices when it comes to Christianity. This is why we have so many denominations throughout America and all over the world. **The most segregated time of the week in America is on Sunday mornings**. This segregation is not only within the church walls, but it's also within the hearts of its congregants. Prejudice and racism have been around for a long time, and God does not condone it. Since we are called to be like Him, we must evaluate, and thus, condemn the prejudice that is at work in our minds when it comes to worship. We must set our hearts to lose this type of filter so we can move to a place of truth.

How many of us prejudge a situation instead of just looking to Jesus? If we're honest, most of us are concerned about the *why* instead of the *Who*.

"Jesus answered and said unto her, If thou knewest the gift of God, and who it is that saith to thee, Give me to drink; thou wouldest have asked of him, and he would have given thee living water" (v. 10).

Jesus is trying to get her to focus on the giver, not the title. If the woman only knew *Whom* she was really talking to, she would see things from a different perspective or filter. If we can truly believe that God is with us in the midst of the situation and believe that, *"All things work together for good to them that love God and are the called according to his purpose" (Romans 8:28)*, then we can surely worship Him in Spirit and in truth.

"The woman saith unto him, Sir, thou hast nothing to draw with, and the well is deep: from whence then hast thou that living water?" (v. 11).

Here, we see her filtering what Jesus said with her own logic. She is trying to make sense, with her mind, of what only her heart can understand. When God speaks something to our hearts, most of the time, we don't understand how it is going to come to pass. Instead of processing what He has said in faith, we often try to process it with our limited experience and understanding. My brothers and sister, we need to lose that filtering process and stop trying to understand God in the light of man's way. If God asks us to do something, He is not asking us to do it in our own strength and understanding. He is asking us to do it from His strength and understanding. *"For [as] the heavens are higher than the earth, so are my ways higher than your ways, and my thoughts than your thoughts" (Isaiah 55:9)*. **God is inviting us to come up and operate where He dwells**.

The woman goes on to say that the well is deep. Now, that will preach. It's no secret that true worship is deep and sometimes incomprehensible. It will allow us to love our enemies, serve when we are tired, and calm our nerves when everything around us is in chaos. Yes, it is deep. When we allow ourselves to go deeper and lose the need to understand everything, when we care more about the living water than we do about the ladle to draw it with, then God can take us to another level.

In the next verse, the Samaritan woman acknowledges how great Jesus is, but she is still trying to figure out why He would want to drink from this well. Jesus has to break it down to show her how much she is relying on her own thoughts and understanding.

"Jesus answered and said unto her, Whosoever drinketh of this water shall thirst again: But whosoever drinketh of the water that I shall give him shall never thirst; but the water that I shall give him shall be in him a well of water springing up into ever-lasting life" (vv.13-14).

Here's a quick scientific fact: as long as we are living, we must continue to put water in our bodies. Water sustains life in our limbs, keeps our organs functioning, and maintains our brains. Worship is like water for our spirit. It's the way we can continually connect with God. When we drink from the water of worship, we won't thirst again because this water will continue to flow out of us. We will always have a continual well of water within. Once we begin to truly worship, we will be able to access God's presence at will.

Letting Go

After Jesus explains this, the woman immediately asks Him for the water that He offers. Finally, she is starting to let go of her filters. She may not understand, but she now desires to never thirst again. Just when breakthrough starts, Jesus decides to go even deeper, revealing yet another one of her filters.

"Jesus saith unto her, Go, call thy husband, and come hither. The woman answered and said, I have no husband. Jesus said unto her, Thou hast well said, I have no husband: For thou hast had five husbands; and he whom thou now hast is not thy husband: in

that saidst thou truly. The woman saith unto him, Sir, I perceive that thou art a prophet" (vv.16-19).

Jesus has now uncovered a filter of her past. He is proving to her that He knows who she is and is not surprised by what she has previously done and is currently doing. For us, this passage means there is no need to hide from God. He knows who we are. Therefore, while we may be concerned with those around us when we come together in worship, the only opinion we should be concerned with is His. We just need to let it go and worship Him.

What things are you holding on to from your past that are preventing you from moving forward with God? What's preventing you from forgiving yourself and others and preventing you from worshipping God in Spirit and in truth?

What about the act of worshipping through praise? Are you apprehensive about lifting your hands? Are you self-conscious when it's time to sing? Do you often feel guilty in His presence? The next time you find yourself in a church service or even alone in your personal worship experience, pay special attention to how you feel when it's time to worship. Then, talk to God about it. Be honest with Him and watch how He leads you to a deeper place in Him.

More Than One Side

It's okay to have filters. This is how we process information so that what we see and hear around us makes sense. We live in a world filled with stimuli that needs processing. That kind of processing turns into our individual experiences and interactions with this place called Earth. This is a part of who we are as human beings on this planet. However, that is only one side of us. We also are a spirit, whose home is in a heavenly place. Therefore, when it comes to worship, which is in the spirit, we have to get rid of the earthly filters that cloud our ultimate expression to the One who gives us life. Regardless of our background, our philosophy, history, or even our mindset, God is looking for the true worshippers who will learn who He is and worship Him in that truth. Remember, He is a Spirit, and so are we. And when our spirits connect with His that is when we experience unfiltered worship.

CHAPTER 12
PREPARATION
GET READY

Let's say a married couple wants a baby. A wife and husband don't simply conceive a child and then not think about the baby until he or she arrives. They go to the doctor to keep up with how the baby is developing while in the womb. They monitor the baby's vitals, making sure he or she is strong and healthy. They are not only checking on the baby while he or she is inside, but they are also making preparations for when the baby will be outside. They get the crib, diapers, wipes, bottles, clothes, a car seat, and all the things they need to keep the baby healthy, happy, protected, and loved. This is what responsible parents do. And just like a husband and wife prepare for the arrival of their child, we, too, must be ready for the mighty things God has meticulously prepared for us.

Anything that is successful, substantial, impactful, and lasting must be preceded with preparation. To *prepare* means to "make something ready for use of service or to get ready for some occasion, test or duty."1 Even God, Himself, prepares. The creation we see all around us is not by happenstance, nor was it made with a *zip bam boom* from a magic wand. God is a thinking God, who takes everything He does into consideration. He took into account, not only what the world would be like, but also what we, the ones who would eventually care for it, would be like. He starts all things with a thought, and this concept and principle now extends to us, the ones whom He calls His children.

Purpose in Preparation

Throughout the Bible, we can find the importance of preparation. God places such a weight on this concept because everything He does has purpose, and **in order for it to have purpose, it must be prepared**. This is no different for you or me, or anyone else we find in the Bible, including Jesus.

God prepared Jesus when Adam and Eve disobeyed Him by eating of the forbidden fruit	*"And I will put enmity between thee and the woman, and between thy seed and her seed; it shall bruise thy head, and thou shalt bruise his heel" (Genesis 3:15).*
God prepared each of His prophets to deliver His message to His chosen people.	*"Before I formed thee in the belly I knew thee; and before thou camest forth out of the womb I sanctified thee, [and] I ordained thee a prophet unto the nations" (Jeremiah 1:5).*
God prepared you and me.	*"According as he hath chosen us in him before the foundation of the world, that we should be holy and without blame before him in love: Having predestinated us unto the adoption of children by Jesus Christ to himself, according to the good pleasure of his will," (Ephesians 1:4-5)*

Foreshadowing

Preparation foreshadows the things that are to come. It is the precursor to the future. Without proper preparation, what lies before us would not exist. Since God is only interested in our success, He has designed a perfect fail-proof plan to prepare us for the things to come. Willingly or unwillingly, we must go through the pre-planned portions of our lives in order to arrive at our expected place of triumph, just as they did in the biblical days.

Out of Abraham's obedience to sacrifice his and Sarah's only promised son, Isaac, there was a foreshadowing of the ultimate sacrifice of Jesus, God's only son.	*"And he said, Lay not thine hand upon the lad, neither do thou any thing unto him: for now I know that thou fearest God, seeing thou hast not withheld thy son, thine only [son] from me" (Genesis 22:12).*
There was a foreshadowing of the holy communion and tithing through Melchizedek when Abram offered the tenth of his possessions to the priest.	*"And Melchizedek king of Salem brought forth bread and wine: and he [was] the priest of the most high God......And blessed be the most high God, which hath delivered thine enemies into thy hand. And he gave him tithes of all" (Genesis 14:18, 20).*
There was a foreshadowing of the difference between the Old and the New Covenant when Moses spoke to the rock instead of smiting it, like he did in Exodus 17:6.	*"Take the rod, and gather thou the assembly together, thou, and Aaron thy brother, and speak ye unto the rock before their eyes; and it shall give forth his water, and thou shalt bring forth to them water out of the rock: so thou shalt give the congregation and their beasts drink" (Numbers 20:8).*
David was prepared in the field, tending the sheep, fighting off the lion and the bear, so he would be ready to trust God to deliver Goliath into his hands.	*"Thy servant slew both the lion and the bear: and this uncircumcised Philistine shall be as one of them, seeing he hath defied the armies of the living God" (1 Samuel 17:36).*
Elisha was an apprentice to Elijah, which prepared him to receive a double portion of Elijah's anointing.	*1 Kings 19:19-21 and 2 Kings 2:6-14.*
Daniel was prepared to show the king that he was stronger, wiser, and more anointed than the younger boys who ate at the king's table, because he had maintained a healthy diet from his youth.	*Daniel 1:12-21.*

Preparation 101

Preparation is the time when faith is born and bred. It is where confidence is created. So many of us have tendencies to do just enough to get by; however, that will never be enough for what God has planned for us. During preparation, our minds and bodies are getting ready to receive the anointing, blessing, supernatural strength, wisdom, and power that we would not be able to handle without that preparation. The cost of being unprepared is too great to pay. This leads to unsuccessful execution, non-impactful results, and an unfulfilled purpose.

Preparation can't be imitated or copied. In the book of Jeremiah (26:20-23), we read about a man named Urijah, who attempted to prophesy according to the words of Jeremiah rather than his own word that he received from the Lord. In other words, he was using someone else's relationship with God to get a Word, instead of his own. Urijah ended up being a target of King Jehoiakim, who wanted to kill him because of his words. He ended up running away to Egypt; however, the king's men eventually found him and killed him. What's the lesson here?

God has given each of us a purpose and has made us all unique. Make sure you speak the word that the Lord has given to you. Urijah tried to walk in Jeremiah's anointing and merely repeated what Jeremiah said. The difference between Urijah's word and Jeremiah's word was that Jeremiah had been prepared to give the word to the people. Urijah had no credibility. Our credibility is lost when we try to convince someone to go through something we have not experienced.

Preparation can't be bought. In the book of Acts, chapter 8, we read about Simon who saw how the apostles had laid hands on people and the Holy Spirit had come upon them. Simon tried to purchase the ability to give the Holy Spirit to other people. Peter quickly set him straight by telling him that the gift of God can't be purchased with money and that his heart was not right. Simon repented immediately.

The world may want to purchase your anointing, but it can't be bought. When you have a gift, people want to own it. They think they can make you compromise yourself so they can own you. God gave you the gift, and your gift will make room for you. You should never have to feel as though you are competing with others over what God has given you to do. People may not blatantly ask how much your anointing costs, but they will want to imitate or search for a formula to obtain it instead of taking the time to prepare themselves in the presence of God. **Take time to know the God Who gives the anointing**.

Preparation is bound to credibility and authority. We see in Acts 19:11-20 that Paul was unusually gifted. A handkerchief he had touched would be placed on people who were sick, and they were instantly healed and delivered. Then, we see, in this example, the Seven Sons of Sceva, who were traveling to different places, casting out evil spirits. They tried to use the name of Jesus by saying, *I command you to come out in the name of Jesus, whom Paul preaches.* At one point, while trying to cast out an evil spirit, it told them that it knew who Jesus was and who Paul was, but it didn't know them, and then proceeded to attack them.

The only way to know someone is by communicating with that person. Paul knew Jesus, and therefore, the evil spirits knew that anyone connected to Jesus has authority over them. The Seven Sons of Sceva were pretending to have authority, but they could not back it up with any power.

You will be able to tell if the Word of God is truly within a person by demonstration and power. Jesus said that we will do greater works than He did. Jesus healed the sick, raised the dead, and cast out demons. If we are going to move to the next level in our walk with Christ, then we must take the time to be prepared. Just like a pot roast needs to sit and cook overnight in seasoning so the juices can merge together, leaving the meat tender and fully prepared, we need to sit in the Word of God during our meditation and allow it to marinate in our spirit.

Count the Cost

The cost of being unprepared can be life changing, risking regression, stagnation, and decrease in our lives. The difference between the prepared and the unprepared is a breakthrough, an answered prayer, deliverance, anointing, and attitude. We all know that our attitude determines our altitude. This is why we prepare our attitude to work in our favor, not against it.

For example, if we're looking for a job, we prepare for the interview; we don't just go in cold turkey. We get our minds focused on the task at hand, entertaining all possible scenarios, just in case we are asked about them. Essentially, we prepare for all things in our lives: to drive, to go to the store, to have a baby, to attend a wedding, to attend a funeral, to go on vacation, etc. We don't do these things arbitrarily. We prepare for the expected and unexpected to the best of our ability. **If we want to be successful, substantial, and impactful, we must put some thought into what we are going to do.**

Preparation may be quite costly if we don't use it wisely. Conversely, it has lucrative dividends when wisely implemented. Preparation is where we:

- learn the purpose behind what we are doing
- make a conscious decision to do something with an expectation of things happening
- gain the faith to follow through
- receive the anointing to do what God has purposed us to do
- have our mind, will, and emotions transformed
- discover that our spirit receives and is made ready

No one said that being prepared would be easy. Like I said, there is a cost. However, we have to stop blaming everybody for the experiences we have or don't have. Even if we are in the midst of our storm, God will speak to us if we open ourselves to hear from Him. If we allow our problems to talk louder than the solution God is giving us, then that is on us. The Bible says to cast down those thoughts and vain imaginations that exalt themselves against the knowledge of God (2 Corinthians 10:5). We have to cast them down. Maybe if we stop speaking doubt and start speaking faith, then we will have what we ask for.

Digest This

Have you made preparations? Have you made plans to come into the presence of the Holy Spirit? If you are asking yourself, why am I here? Why don't I feel anything? You simply haven't prepared yourself to receive anything. I guarantee that if you take some time to prepare your mind, attitude, will, and emotions and then pray, seeking the face of God, you will not come out disappointed or confused. Instead, you will have clarity and purpose.

Prepared to Eat

Preparation is necessary, and it begins in the prayer closet. Do you want to know your purpose in life? Prepare yourself so God can show you during your prayer time with Him. He wants to prepare us to receive everything He has for us. He first wants to prepare our hearts and minds to deal with our weaknesses, to conquer the little giants before big ones arise. This comes when we are alone with Him. **If we are not prepared to go to the next level in our lives, now is the time to get in our prayer closet and shut the door.**

There's a principle at work: if we can't be consistent in our alone-time with God, we will not be consistent in being used by Him to help someone in need. If we can't be consistent in giving, we will be ill prepared to receive a monetary blessing. Everything we do, every decision we make, affects our future. As we all know, a wrong decision can cause a lifetime of pain. However, a right decision can cause a lifetime of joy. It is all a continual process.

"But you, when you pray, go into your room, and when you have shut your door, pray to your Father who [is] in the secret [place]; and your Father who sees in secret will reward you openly" (Matthew 6:6, NKJV)

I encourage you to take inventory and ask yourself *Am I prepared?* Are you really prepared to be healed, set free, and delivered? Are you prepared for a financial breakthrough? Are you prepared for that new job, that new car, or a new house? Are you prepared to begin a new relationship or raise a family? Are you prepared for the unexpected?

Preparation doesn't happen overnight. With each moment you spend with God, you create a bank account that you can draw on in your time of need as you live your life. So what is holding you back from embarking on this journey? If you are reading this book, then you are serious about raising the standard in your spiritual life. You are dedicated to growth and development in your spirit. You are willing to examine yourself, inspect your life, and discover clues about your life that have led you to this point—things to remember as you go through this journey. Be an active participant in your life. Don't let life just happen to you. If you feel as though you have messed up, use your mistakes as your message, your slip-up as your sermon, your wondering as your wakeup call. Yes, it's time to wake up, grow up, put up, or shut up. You only have one life to live and one lifetime to live it. I don't know about you, but I don't want to do just enough to get by. I want to see how far I can go and stretch myself to my limits, and then I want the limits to be removed. Sure, we can live up to or down to everyone else's expectation of us, but when we get a glimpse of God's expectation for our lives, we open ourselves up to the journey. We open ourselves up to things that are beyond our comprehension.

No one can walk out our journey for us, and there is no set map for the journey. We must create this journey as we go along, with or without the resources available to us. Are you ready to truly take ownership of your journey? It may seem like a lot to digest, but the way to successfully complete the journey we are on is by taking one day at a time and living equipped with God's power and His Word.

Endnotes

Chapter 1
1 https://www.harding.edu/gclayton/a475_intro.html. Accessed 1/26/2018.
2Ibid.
3Ibid.

Chapter 2
1 https://www.blueletterbible.org/lang/Lexicon/Lexicon.cfm?strongs=H5104&t=KJV. Accessed 3/18/2017.

Chapter 3
1 https://www.blueletterbible.org/lang/Lexicon. Accessed 3/18/2017.
2 Ibid.
3Ibid.
4Ibid.

Chapter 5
1https://www.merriam-webster.com. Accessed 4/12/2017.

Chapter 7
1 www.dictionary.com/browse/google. Accessed 3/25/2017

Chapter 12
1https://www.merriam-webster.com. Accessed 4/25/2017.